Sub-regional Cooperation in South Asia: India, Sri Lanka and Maldives

Sub-regional Cooperation in South Asia: India, Sri Lanka and Maldives

Editors

Venugopal B. Menon and Joshy M. Paul

Vij Books India Pvt Ltd

New Delhi (India)

Published by

Vij Books India Pvt Ltd
(Publishers, Distributors & Importers)
2/19, Ansari Road
Delhi – 110 002
Phones: 91-11-43596460, 91-11-47340674
Fax: 91-11-47340674
e-mail: vijbooks@rediffmail.com
web: www.vijbooks.com

Contents

Preface

South Asia had, over a long period, been depicted as a region of poverty and hunger, nuclear instability, political rivalry between India and Pakistan, and religious extremism. It has launched regional grouping mechanism, called South Asian Association for Regional Cooperation (SAARC), in the 1980s to emulate the success of Southeast Asian region and create the region as a vibrant and cohesive unit. However, the everlasting issue of Kashmir dispute and historical baggage of 'two nation theory', India and Pakistan have not been able make the relationship normal. This has spoiled the region to implement various initiatives adopted for regional integration process such as South Asian Free Trade Area (SAFTA). In fact, economic integration process contributes political stability but the lacks of strong economic engagement between the member countries hamper the region to become a vibrant regional grouping.

India has initiated earlier to create a sub-regional mechanism in the east for the economic development of the north east. Various ministers and government officials propounded the idea of 'look east through north east' to reap the economic benefit of India's look east policy for the land locked northeastern region bringing seven northeastern states and the Southeast Asian countries. It also proposed a trans-continental Asian highway linking India, Myanmar, and Thailand through a road system stretching 3,200 kilometers from Moreh in India to Thailand's Maesot. However, there is no such proposal for connectivity on the maritime front in the sub-continent, while coordination on the maritime security front is more on piecemeal basis. Although Sri Lanka and Maldives have been included in Asian Development Bank's South Asia Subregional Economic Cooperation project along with India, Bangladesh, Bhutan and Nepal in 2014, but the focus is still in land connectivity. The two island nations of Sri Lanka and Maldives and the southern peninsula of India face identical, though not similar, issues from the sea, such as piracy, impact of climate change, and maritime terrorism. Importantly, China's maritime expansion towards the

Indian Ocean Region (IOR) is posing major security challenge for India. It is imperative for India to consider sub-regional grouping comprising India, Sri Lanka and Maldives for the promotion of India's national interest as well as regional prosperity.

In this regard, Department of International Studies and History, School of Law, Christ University, Bangalore organized a two day conference on the theme "Sub-regional Cooperation in South Asia: India, Sri Lanka and Maldives" on August 31-September 1, 2015 at the Christ University Auditorium. The seminar discussed main issues which affect the region such as piracy and other forms of non-traditional security issues, economic issues, political problems, China's role in the Indian Ocean and its impact on India, and suggested various mechanisms to improve the interaction between the three nations. The Christ University provided financial and logistical support to conduct the seminar.

We are extremely thankful to the management of the University, especially the Honourable Vice Chancellor, Pro-Vice Chancellor, the Finance Officer, the Registrar, Director and Dean, School of Law, faculties of Department of International Studies and History, and other fraternities of the Christ University. We also express our gratitude to Ms. Sandra Kuriakose and her team in helping organizing the event successfully. We express our gratitude to the students also who presented the papers in the seminar which are unfortunately not included in this book.

Venugopal B. Menon & Joshy M. Paul

Abbreviations

ALH	Advanced Light Helicopter
AIADMK	All India Dravida Munnetra Kazhagam
ADD	Annual Defence Dialogue
APEC	Asia Pacific Economic Cooperation
ADB	Asian Development Bank
ASEAN	Association of Southeast Asian Nations
AIS	Automatic Identification system
BCIM	Bangladesh, China, India, Myanmar
BIMSTEC	Bangladesh, India, Myanmar, Sri Lanka Technical Co-operation
BCE	Before Common Era
CFA	Ceasefire Agreement
CENTO	Central Treaty Organisation
CHEC	China Harbour Engineering Company
CMEC	China Machinery Engineering Corporation
CUP	China Union Pay
CTC	Combating Terrorism Center
CEPA	Comprehensive Economic Partnership Agreement
CGPCS	Contact Group on Piracy off the Coast of Somalia
DCA	Defence Cooperation Agreement
DMK	Dravida Munnetra Kazhagam
EEF	Emergency Economic Fund

EU	European Union
EEZ	Exclusive Economic Zone
FET	Faculty of Engineering Technology
IMFFHTS	Faculty of Hospitality & Tourism Studies)
FDI	Foreign Direct Investment
FTA	Free Trade Agreement
IGMH	Gandhi Memorial Hospital
GDP	Gross Domestic Product
GEP	Group of Eminent Persons
HADR	Humanitarian Assistance and Disaster Relief
ICC	India Cultural Center
IAF	Indian Air Force
ICG	Indian Coast Guard
IONS	Indian Ocean Naval Symposium
IOR	Indian Ocean Region
IORA	Indian Ocean Rim Association
IOR-ARC	Indian Ocean Rim–Association for Regional Cooperation
IPKF	Indian Peace Keeping Force (IPKF)
ISFTA	India-Sri Lanka Free Trade Agreement
IMBL	International Maritime Boundary Line
IBRD	International Bank for Reconstruction and Development
IDA	International Development Association
IFR	International Fleet Review
IMO	International Maritime Organisation
ITLOS	International Tribunal on the Law of the Sea

IFM	Islamic Foundation of Maldives
JS	Jamiyyathu Salaf
JVP	Janatha Vimukthi Peramuna
JHU	Jatika Hela Urumuya
JOC	Joint Operations Centres
L&T	Larsen & Toubro
LeT	Lashkar –e –Taiba
LTTE	Liberation Tigers of Tamil Eelam
LRIT	Long Range Information and Tracking
MDP	Maldivian Democratic Party
MNDF	Maldivian National Defense Forces
MDA	Maritime Domain Awareness
MRCCs	Maritime Rescue Coordination Centres
MSR	Maritime Silk Road
MOU	Memorandum of Understanding
MSIS	Merchant Ship Information System
MOOTW	Military Operations other than War
MOD	Ministry of Defence
MoES	Ministry of Earth Sciences
MEA	Ministry of External Affairs
NMA	National Maritime Authority
NC³I	National Command, Control, Communication and Intelligence
NDA	National Democratic Alliance
NSA	National Security Advisor
NTPC	National Thermal Power Corporation
NAM	Non Alignment Movement

NAFTA	North America Free Trade Agreement
OPV	Offshore Support Vessels
PIA	Pakistani International Airlines
PLA	People's Liberation Army
PLOTE	People's Liberation Organisation of Tamil Eelam
PMSC	Private Maritime Security Companies
RCI	Regional Cooperation and Integration
RAW	Research and Analysis Wing
SAAPTA	SAARC Preferential Trading Arrangement
SLOC	Sea Lanes of Communication
SAR	Search and Rescue
SIDS	Small Island Developing States
SAARC	South Asian Association of Regional Cooperation
SAFTA	South Asian Free Trade Agreement
SASEC	South Asian Sub-Regional Economic Cooperation
SEATO	Southeast Asia Treaty Organisation
SLMM	Sri Lanka Monitoring Mission
SIMI	Students Islamic Movement of India
USSR	Union of Soviet Socialist Republic
UNCLOS	United Nations Conference on the Laws of the Seas
UAV	Unmanned Aerial Vehicles
VBSS	Visit, Board, Search and Seizure
WTO	World Trade Organisation

List of Contributors

Venugopal B. Menon is Professor, Department of International Studies and History, School of Law, Christ University, Bangalore.

Joshy M. Paul is an Assistant Professor, Department of International Studies and History, School of Law, Christ University, Bangalore.

Ashik J. Bonofer is an Assistant Professor, Department of Political Science Madras Christian College, Tambaram, Chennai.

M. Mayilvaganan is an Assistant Professor in International Strategic and Security Studies programme at National Institute of Advanced Studies (NIAS), Indian Institute of Science campus, Bangalore.

P K Ghosh is presently a Senior Fellow at the Observer Research Foundation (ORF). He was the coordinator of the major Indian maritime initiative IONS (Indian Ocean Naval Symposium) held in 2008. He was the Co Chair and India representative to two consecutive CSCAP International Study Groups on Maritime Security.

Shaji. S is an Assistant Professor in the Department of Political Science at University of Hyderabad, Hyderabad.

T.C.Karthikheyan teaches International Relations and Political Science at the Tamil Nadu Open University, Chennai.

P.M. Heblikar is Managing Trustee, Institute of Contemporary Studies Bangalore (ICSB) and former Special Secretary, Government of India.

Anand P. Mavalankar is Professor, Department of Political Science, Faculty of Arts, M.S. University of Baroda.

Jiss Tom Palelil is Research Associate, Department of International Studies and History, School of Law, Christ University, Bangalore.

S.Y. Surendra Kumar is an Assistant Professor, Department of Political Science, Bangalore University, Bangalore.

V. Suryanarayan is a retired Professor and founding Director, Centre for South and Southeast Asian Studies, University of Madras, and is one of India's leading specialists in South and Southeast Asian Studies. He is currently associated with two think tanks in Chennai; the Center for Asia Studies and the Chennai Centre for China Studies.

Udai Rao is a retired Commodore from Indian Navy. He is a former Principal Director Naval Intelligence (PDNI) and has served in the Cabinet Secretariat, Government of India.

Anurag Tripathi is an Assistant Professor, Department of International Studies and History, School of Law, Christ University, Bangalore.

Chapter 1

Introduction: Sub-regional Cooperation in South Asia

Joshy M. Paul

Introduction

Sub-regional cooperation can be seen in many parts of the world which has been formed either to make a particular region's emancipation from underdevelopment or utilizing the comparative economic advantage of a specific geographical area. The sub regional cooperation, both intra and extra-regional, has contributed national gross domestic product (GDP) as well as to the regional economic development, which in turn helped the regional integration process. It aims to exploit complementarities between geographically contiguous areas of different countries to gain a comparative edge in production for export, utilizing market and creation of political cohesiveness in the region. Thus, the sub-regional cooperation that straddles national boundaries is making a major contribution to growth and stability in the region.

Sovereign states seek to pursue regional integration process only when their national interests are compatible with the regional integration goal. In the regional integration process it is the interest of the individual states which tries to get maximum advantage while losing some of the benefits it currently enjoys. The regional integration process involves a series of bargains between the heads of governments of the state in a region. Nation-states ensure balance between national interest and regional interest while searching for regional integration goal. Indeed, domestic consideration plays a critical role in shaping the nature and scope of regional integration process.

Sub-regional cooperation can become a catalyst for larger regional integration process also. If the whole regional countries could not come together because of ideological or politico-security issues then sub regional cooperation of countries with commonalities will play significant role in the regional integration process. It can initially begin with economic cooperation at the sub regional level then can expand into a political one. The sub-regional economic cooperation concept has taken hold because it is a controlled experiment in regional cooperation whose adverse effects, if any, can be limited to the triangle, but whose beneficial results can subsequently be applied to the national economy as a whole. It offers the benefits of regional integration without great loss of economic sovereignty. The greatest benefits accrue to the most industrially mature partner. But even the poorest partner gains in practical terms as a result of job generation, skills development, technology transfer and the infusion of industrial discipline in the local work force. Once economic cooperation is fructified then it can convert into political cooperation.

Scope and structure of sub-regional cooperation are substantially influenced by a number of factors such as political and institutional components, economic factors and developments in trade relations[1]. Since South Asia region has not emerged as a political and security institutions like European Union or Southeast Asia, economic factors still play a predominant role in the sub regional cooperation which will help in establishing better political cooperation. Main economic factors are: firstly, the level of sub-regional cooperation depends on the *size* of the available regional market. However, it is important that the market size depends on purchasing power as well as population. Market mechanism provides strong incentives to production and trade within the sub-regional area, while lesser demand becomes a constraint for companies operating in the region.

Secondly, *level of economic development* is another aspect on sub-regional cooperation. The higher this is, the more fields open for sub-regional cooperation. On the one hand, higher development leads to higher disposable income, and so to a larger market. On the other, intra industry specialization develops, creating a more sophisticated division of labour among group members. *Geographical orientation and openness* is the third factor which strongly affect the scope of sub-regional cooperation. Economic openness and world market orientation incline a group to a higher level of regional cooperation. The opposite applies to inward looking countries engaged in national or regional import substitution.

Fourthly, *initial conditions* may affect the propensity to sub-regional cooperation and the efficiency of it. If countries pursue ideology based economic policies to protect its domestic market, then it will not be easy for them to open up the economy for competition. It will be a gradual process of privatization, liberalisation and competition at the domestic front. And, finally, sub-regional cooperation correlates positively with *similar economic policies* in participating countries. This similarity may result from coordinated economic policies, or from global (and larger regional) impacts on open economies.

Sub-regional cooperation attaches great importance to the share of intra-regional trade in total trade of the regional countries. Trade is clearly one of the most manifested quantitative indicators, often used as a composite figure to cover, if indirectly, the impact on regional cooperation of economic policies, FDI, technological advancement and institutional relations. Newer integration trends, based on the concept and reality of the new regionalism, have ceased to take intra-regional trade as the sole, or even the main indicator of sub-regional cooperation.[2] Increasing attention is paid to other factors; political cooperation, social interpenetration, cultural links, and other economic aspects like coordination of competition, exchange rates, and monetary and other policies. It helps to institutionalize the sub-regional integration process more effectively.

Foreign Direct Investment (FDI) may have a substantial impact on sub-regional contacts as it brings new technology, management methods, products and mentality into the host country, creating a' harmonization network' in the sub-region.[3] The investors may be from within the sub-region or from the region or even from outside the region. It enhances growth and increases market opportunities for the products produced within the sub-region. It generates production structures that promote intra-industry as well as intra-regional trade. Growing investment, foreign and domestic, is likely to create new development poles that may link regions in different countries. This tendency can be seen in Western Europe and Southeast Asia.

In fact, sub-regional integration is a stepping stone to membership of a larger framework. Since their markets are small, so they are depended on outside their immediate geographical area. Less developed countries need large markets (in population and purchasing power), access to technology, capital and managerial know how, so does it requires a moderation anchor in the form of a big regional country. For instance, Japan played an anchoring role for the Southeast Asian countries; Portugal and Spain have depended on EU, especially Germany. In the Asian case, the sub-regional mechanism has been evolved to utilise the locally available resources such as land, labour and natural resources and exported the semi or finished products to the outside market. It has contributed higher growth, higher income and more differentiated production based on a global division of labour that created conditions for sub-regional cooperation.

It can be seen in Eastern Europe and the Baltic Sea region, and also in other parts of Asia, sub-regional cooperation has brought not only economic development but increased political connectivity among the member countries. For instance, the "Southern Growth Triangle" (SIJORI), formed in 1989, comprising Singapore, Johor in Malaysia and the Indonesian island of Batam in the province of Riau has helped to mitigate the territorial dispute between the three countries and also emerged as the model of various growth triangles in the region. Similarly, six countries — Cambodia, Laos, Myanmar, Thailand, Vietnam and China (Yunnan province) — have formed Greater Mekong Sub region (GMS) which was initiated in the early 1990s, well after SAARC was born. Supported by the Asian Development Bank (ADB), GMS galvanised a natural economic community on the banks of the Mekong River. The establishment of a power grid GMS shares as well as an optical fibre network connecting the regional countries with Yunnan province helps the understanding of the regional engagement between the 'Big Brother' and small neighbours without any hiccups.

The eight countries grouping of the South Asian Association for Regional Cooperation (SAARC) is a combination of various political regimes, socio-economic realities, ethnic differentials, religious and linguistic diversity the world could possibly offer. As a result, a regional integration scheme with several states, their clashing ideologies, values and interests, and national/domestic policies, makes it difficult in its efforts to bring regional integration in South Asia. Also, it has been stymied by the political tension between India and Pakistan. The South Asian Free Trade Area (SAFTA) has now become a non-existent entity. In this regard, a sub-regional cooperation among the island nations of the northern Indian Ocean countries such as Sri Lanka and Maldives and India would provide the much needed fillip to the lack of regional integration in South Asia.

Regional cooperation in South Asia

Ever since SAARC was formed in 1985, it registered modest gains in the first few years due to the shadow of the cold war in the region. Liberalised tariff regime and market oriented trade activities are integral to the concept of regionalism. However, the domestic economic policy of most of the South Asian countries was not conducive to facilitate trade oriented activities. While regionalism in other parts of the world was a beneficiary of political proximity of generations of leadership, robust private sector companies transcending national borders and multinational stakeholders that facilitated regional cohesiveness. However, the template of political interaction in South Asia, and the contours of interface between the governments and non-governmental stakeholders, including the private sector and think-tanks, is far more complex. The functional cooperation in South Asia has largely been dependent on cordiality of relations among the political elites, so that focus of the interaction among the regional countries has by and large been political in nature.

The regional countries have initiated economic liberalization and deregulation in the 1990s which should have created a conducive atmosphere for increased interaction, as action in the economic field moved out of government control. India, Sri Lanka, Bangladesh and Pakistan registered impressive growth indices in the following decades. However, the spurt of globalization had shifted their priorities from looking into regional advantage to getting maximum benefit out of the globalised world. At the same time, lack of regional connectivity, issue of governance and bureaucratic inertia made hindrance to the evolutionary process of the regionalism in South Asia. In a way the regional elites did not give enough attention to steadying the regional integration both economically as well as politically.

One of the key structural impediments to strengthening of regional economic cooperation in South Asia is lack of physical and soft connectivity. Infrastructure constraints like power shortages, underdeveloped road and rail network, port congestion, etc. seriously hinder full realization of the regional trade potential. It is now acknowledged that reduction in transport and infrastructure-related costs has the same effect as tariff liberalization in providing stimulus to trade[4]. It is estimated that for every one per cent reduction in cost, trade stimulus is about 5 per cent. This benefit is passed along the entire supply chain, be they shippers, truckers, traders or end-users. Another illustration of deficiencies in soft connectivity is that only 7 per cent of international calls in South Asia are in the region, whereas in East Asia the corresponding figure is 71 per cent[5]. Studies on regional cooperation has showed that it accrue economic benefits for all, particularly to smaller countries, through better trade and economic cooperation.

In order to enhance regional trade and better connectivity, regional countries formed SAFTA (South Asian Free Trade Agreement) in 2004 which eventually came into force in 2006. It showed a way forward despite lingering bilateral issues between India and Pakistan. Since SAFTA Trade Liberalisation Programme was launched in 2006, total trade under SAFTA certificates of origin reached to $3 billion in 2013 (Sept) from $687 million in 2009. However, Intra SAARC trade continues to be very low (at about 5 per cent of the region's total trade), and India's imports from rest of South Asia is less than 1% of its total imports. In this context it is important that a sub regional cooperation between India, Sri Lanka and Maldives can become a role model for larger South Asian regional cooperation.

Importance of sub-regionalism in South Asia

Sub-regional cooperation can be seen in Eastern Europe, the Baltic Sea region, and in Asia, as it has brought not only economic development but increased political connectivity among the member countries also. For instance, the "Southern Growth Triangle" (SIJORI), formed in 1989, comprising Singapore, Johor in Malaysia and the Indonesian island of Batam in the province of Riau has helped to mitigate the territorial dispute between the three countries and also emerged as the model of various growth triangles in the region. Similarly, six countries — Cambodia, Laos, Myanmar, Thailand, Vietnam and China (Yunnan province) — have formed Greater Mekong Sub region (GMS) which was initiated in the early 1990s, well after SAARC was born. Supported by the Asian Development Bank (ADB), GMS galvanized a natural economic community on the banks of the Mekong River. The establishment of a power grid GMS shares as well as an optical fiber network connecting the regional countries with Yunnan province, helps the understanding of the regional engagement between the 'Big Brother' and small neighbours without any hiccups.

A South Asian Growth Quadrangle (SAGQ) was mooted in SAARC council of ministers held in New Delhi in May 1996, consisting of Bangladesh, Bhutan, Nepal, India's north-eastern region (Arunachal Pradesh, Assam, Manipur, Meghalaya, Mizoram, Nagaland, Tripura and Sikkim) and West Bengal, but was almost shelved in the next SAARC Summit held at Male in May 1997. After that another sub-regional grouping was initiated, known as South Asia Sub-Regional Cooperation (SA-SRC), focusing on Climate Adaptation and Agriculture in South Asia, and also joint capacity building program. However, the climate adaptation mechanism of the continental countries such as Pakistan, Nepal, Bhutan and continental India are different from the challenges facing the impact of climate change among island nations such as Maldives as well as the peninsular India. For them, increasing sea level due to the climate change is a challenging issue. At the same time, road or rail connectivity will enhance the trade between Himalayan countries whereas for oceanic trade it requires efficient ports and shipping mechanism.

There has been a growing perception that India has chosen to ignore the island nations in the context of an India-Pak stalemate. Similarly the closer linkage of economic and foreign policy has more focused towards the East Asian region in the post liberalization period. The newly 'assertive' foreign policy which include the 'look-east' policy, now the so called 'act-east' policy has brought India more closer to the Asia-pacific region which further caused to ignore the importance of regionalism in South Asia. However, China's increasing influence in the Indian Ocean region and its various infrastructure facilities, known as 'string of pearls', necessitated New Delhi to focus on the island nations. It is imperative for New Delhi that Sri Lanka or Maldives should never come under the strategic influence of Beijing. Since the LTTE problems are resolved and Sri Lanka needs India's support for its economic development, a sub-regional cooperation will enhance the bilateral relationship too.

Although India is the largest trading partner of Sri Lanka but the total trade between the two in 2015-16 is $ 6.05 billion which accounts just 0.0.94 per cent of India's total trade. Maldives accounts 0.03 per cent of India's total trade but India's economic presence in Maldives is remarkable. The

India-Sri Lanka Free Trade Agreement signed on March 2000 has provided a big boost in bilateral trade which multiplied nearly five-fold over the next decade. However, the economic interaction between South India and the island nations, as the region comes in contiguously advantageous area, is very minimal. Trade and investment between them need to be improved.

In many ways, India considered the regional mainland connectivity with the island nations as part of its larger diplomacy, and also the neighboring countries looking upon India for some of its essential materials. The post tsunami humanitarian relief operation and economic assistance by various Indian agencies to the island nations were able to build trust and confidence among the people. However, more functional cooperation in other areas which include science and technology, disaster management, human resource capacity development, and maritime security can play a vital role in bringing regional integration in South Asia.

The South Asian countries are members of the Indian Ocean Regional Association (IORA), and interact at various stages under the IORA, but a sub-regional cooperation will enhance the growth potential of entire region. Scholars like Kishore C Das argue 'export oriented growth' as a panacea to build successful institutional mechanism for integration and cooperation. Indeed, several other regions have started to engage in political or security cooperation at a fairly late stage in the life of their respective framework organizations, which were originally set up with aims of trade and development promotion. Starting with a localized step to construct a wider regional regime of confidence building, transparency and openness, would be a more favorable approach to keep regionalism progressed. Peninsular India-island economic cooperation could lead to functional engagement, which in turn, helps stabilize the political cooperation in the entire South Asia. In this regard this book tries to explain the importance of sub-regional cooperation in South Asia comprising India, Sri Lanka and Maldives as well as various mechanisms of cooperation that have been developed at different stages which include economic, political and security wise. It will also explain the nuances of regional security issues.

The book is divided into 13 chapters. Ashik J Bonofer explains that India's relations with Sri Lanka and Maldives has not always been cordial, rather it is more of love and hate relationship depending on the scenario and time. Since all of them became independent after the end of the World War II, enmity has never developed in the relationship as was in the case of

Pakistan or Bangladesh. He has identified that geographical and economic asymmetry is the major reasons for imbalance and conflict in South Asia. Conflict between India and Pakistan; India and Bangladesh; strained economic relations between India and Nepal; India and Bhutan and uneasy relations between India and Sri Lanka; India and Maldives are visible signs of problems in asymmetrical relations in South Asia. However, in recent times India has taken the initiative to bring the two island nations in its fold to counter the threat of Jihadi fundamentalism and Chinese expansionism in the Indian Ocean region. Importantly, these countries are vital cog in the aspect of India's security interest.

M. Mayilvaganan argues that Sri Lanka and Maldives share historical, cultural, religious, ethnic and linguistic links with India. All the ethnic groups in these island nations are in one or other way considered being from India in every sense because of the geographical proximity, cultural and religious linkage process. Nonetheless, this proximity had played a part in forcing them—Sri Lankan and Maldivians—to exhibit that they are 'distinct.' The ruling elites desire to shed away their 'Indian-ness' is an effort to defend and promote their own 'identity' which is essential for their existence. In this chapter he analyses various kinds of linkages the two island nations carry with India and explains the importance of coming closer them each other.

P. K.Ghosh analyses various aspects of maritime cooperation of India, Sri Lanka and Maldives. According to him cooperation in the maritime security arena using modern technology in capacity building is a relatively new concept in the Indian Ocean region. For India, a primary maritime power in the region and a net security provider, it is relatively an innovative concept. At the same time new challenges such as piracy and maritime terrorism as well as external powers increasing influence in the region, it is imperative for India to enhance maritime cooperation with the neighboring island nations.

Shaji. S explains that Sub-regional cooperation could tide over certain macro-level constraints which hamper the South Asian regional frame work. An effective sub-regional cooperation will improve trade and development cooperation which will benefit politically also because many macro level constraints emanate out of longstanding political conflicts in the region. He further argues that there are many ways through which states in South Asia try to improve relations as evident from the increased dynamism in signing bilateral and trilateral arrangements. China and India will compete to acquire more opportunities of trade and business, along with achieving a high degree of strategic depth in the Indian Ocean region. In his opinion, increased trilateral cooperation in trade and development would create a regional political economy in South Asia.

T. C.Karthikheyan in his essay politics among the South Asian troika explains that South Asia as a region in terms of international relations and regional politics has always been the connoisseur of big power politics. The South Asian region has recently gained prominence when US launched rebalancing strategy towards Asia Pacific region. In this context, relations among the South Asian states necessitate regular evaluation and updating for the betterment of the millions of people who live in this region. Since SAARC has been able provide the regional identity, a sub-regional grouping could provide a supporting role in the rebalancing strategy. The chapter also looks into the importance of the sub regional political engagements among India, Sri Lanka and Maldives and its implications on the political, economic and security aspects.

P.M. Heblikar analyses the political developments in Sri Lanka and its impact on regional security dynamics. He emphasizes that when regime change happens in Sri Lanka it affects the island nation's relationship with India. Former President Mahinda Rajpaksa's inept handling of the minority issues was a cause of concern, as had paid little attention to India's concern as far as Tamilians are concerned. The reconciliation efforts are underway under the new dispensation and President Maitripala Sirisena has embarked on several confidence building measures in keeping with his election promises especially the desire to bring about constitutional and political reforms. Once internal political order is established in Sri Lanka, then more fruitful cooperation can be achieved in the region.

In his essay Mavalankar deals with political economic aspects of the sub-regional cooperation. He says that like the 'look-east' policy, India must look towards the 'south' also. He explains India's cooperative efforts to build a strong foundation of Indo-Sri Lankan and Indo-Maldivian strategic and economic relations in contemporary times. His chapter examines complementarities between geographically contiguous areas of countries, especially in regard to comparative advantage in exports, and also analyzes the broad question of growth and stability in the region.

Jiss Tom analyses the impact of China's maritime silk route in the sub-regional cooperation especially between India and Sri Lanka. He says that

China's increasing involvement will create a situation in which a friction could occur between China and India in terms of political, diplomatic, economic and strategic aspects. The race to dominate the Indian Ocean region, which is strategically important to both, can be quoted as a typical example for this endeavour for domination. In this regard, his chapter is an attempt to explore the power relations between both the countries in the India Ocean region.

Surendra Kumar says that the rise of China is attributed to various factors like rapid economic growth; strategic modernization; reconnecting with the Chinese diaspora, particularly in the west; modernization of its military; and vibrant maritime trade strategy. As a result, China has emerged as an important shareholder in global governance and international security. In the process, the China's rise has also led to its growing influence in various regions around the world. In this regard, South Asia is no different, as China has successfully intensified its engagements with South Asian region through strong economic, military and political relations with countries like Pakistan, Bangladesh, Nepal, Sri Lanka and Maldives. Furthermore, China is also making its presence felt in the region in different multinational foras. He argues that China's increasing economic, diplomatic and military power in South Asia is influencing India's security strategies towards the South Asia region.

V. Suryanarayan analyses diversities and linkages that exhibits in the region. He says that all the three countries have commonalities in many areas such as threat perceptions, both internal and external, identity of political systems, common foreign policy stances on crucial global issues, and an unwritten understanding of the role of pivotal power – India in the case of South Asia – which provides internal cohesion and lessening of inter-state tensions in the region. Similarly, there has been a strong cultural linkage between the people among the three countries. Some of the ancient writings, regarding both Hindus and non-Hindus, from India talks about the culture of Sri Lanka and Maldives. This cultural linkage can be utilized for better political cooperation.

Udai Rao analyses the impact of India's maritime security policy and cooperative mechanism to face the challenges emanating in the maritime front. He says that the Indian Ocean has today emerged as the center of gravity of the world in the maritime domain and India becomes the centrality in the Indian Ocean strategic arena. India has for long period been obsessed with Pakistan and neglected other close neighbor's, specially the small island nations in the Indian Ocean. However in the last decade the China factor has emerged as a cause for concern – the 'String of Pearls Strategy', the New Maritime Silk Route (NMSR), the foray of Chinese submarines, etc, all on the back of Chinese 'Cheque Book Diplomacy' do not portend well for India. Today, India and the island nation face common threat in the maritime front such as terrorism, piracy, and Islamic fundamentalism as they have been using sea as a safe route to cross the border. In the regard Udai Rao explains various mechanisms which can be adopted by the three countries so that cooperation will become steadier.

Anurag Tripathi explains the challenges sub-regional countries face, especially Maldives. He argues that one of the major problems Maldives faces on fundamentalism is that the expatriates carry ideology of fundamentalism to the island nation. Those people who have gone to Pakistan and Saudi Arabia for education purposes are being indoctrinated with fundamentalism and they propound it in the home country. Similarly, Saudi and Pakistani funds have made schools, mosques and university grants available to Maldivian citizens, exposing them to more radical interpretations of familiar texts. Although India's soft power diplomacy has made quite success in propagating the menaces of Islamic fundamentalism, the political instability still plays the spoilsport.

Endnotes

1   Andras Inatoi, "Correlations between European Integration and Sub-regional Cooperation: Theoretical Background, Experience and Policy Impacts", Russian and East European Finance and Trade, Vol 34, No. 6, 1998. Pp. 3-91.

2   Ibid

3   Inatoi, "Correlations between European Integration and Sub-regional Cooperation

4   Jörn Dosch and Oliver Hensengerth, "Sub-Regional Cooperation in Southeast Asia: The Mekong Basin", European Journal of East Asian Studies, Vol. 4, No. 2 ,2005, pp. 263-285

5   Prabhu Ghate, "The Institutions of Regionalism in South Asia—Do Institutions Matter?", *Asian Development Bank*, 2011. P.

Chapter 2

India-Sri Lanka-Maldives: The Problem of Asymmetry in the Sub-regional Cooperation

Ashik J Bonofer

Sub-regional cooperation is a dream comes true for South Asia. India since independence has been bound by evasive relations with its southern neighbours who are keen on avoiding any relations with her if provided with an opportunity. For both Sri Lanka and Maldives, India is not only the closest neighbour but also a big bullying brother. It is surprising India as to why its neighbours have been unhappy with New Delhi, despite providing them with critical support at crucial times, be it during the tsunami of 2004, the ethnic conflict in Sri Lanka since the 1970s, or the *coup d'état* in Maldives in 1988. India went out of her way to support her island neighbours. In some instances we were considered as the last resort. It is debatable as to who should be blamed for these uneasy relations. Why are these countries scared of India? Has India been an aggressor in the past? Does India continue to interfere in the affairs of the Maldives and Sri Lanka? How do extra-regional powers react?

India's relations with Sri Lanka and Maldives cannot be categorised as cordial; rather it is more of a love and hate relation depending on the scenario and time. Unlike Pakistan and Bangladesh, which were partitioned from India, Sri Lanka and Maldives have always been independent states. Even during the colonial rule both these countries were considered independent entities. Hence, one can affirm that India's experience with these countries have not been on a sub-regional scale but at an individual level.

The Problem of Asymmetry in South Asia

Understanding of an asymmetrical relationship is moulded within the premise that any nation that is generally powerful is capable of disproportionately imposing its will on the other and setting conditions, making decisions, taking action and exercising control which is determinative of the relationship.[1] This scenario is commonly witnessed in day to day activities among people and nations as well. The Cold War politics, race for supremacy since the end of Cold War, the US acting as the world super cop, China's political and strategic dominance in Asia are all examples of asymmetrical relations. Observing on similar lines, geographical and economic asymmetry are the major reasons for imbalance and conflict in South Asia. Conflict between India and Pakistan, India and Bangladesh, strained economic relations between India and Nepal, India and Bhutan, uneasy relations between India and Sri Lanka, and India and Maldives are visible signs of problems in asymmetrical relations in South Asia. One cannot ignore the failures of South Asian Association of Regional Cooperation (SAARC), or SAARC becoming a victim of restrained relations in South Asia. It is an open secret that a majority of the South Asian countries consider India to be a big bullying brother. Despite India's repeated commitments to respecting other countries' sovereignty and adopting principles such as the Gujral doctrine, smaller neighbours still fear Indian intentions. Ever since the British vacated South Asia, all the smaller countries have tried to attract the attention of extra regional forces into regional affairs. During the Cold War it was the Americans and the West. Since the dawn of the present century, China has become the favourite. The String of Pearls strategy is the icing on the cake.

Another important trend one witnesses in South Asia is the growing influence of Pakistan. Unlike China, which financially twists the arms of smaller countries to accept their stand, Pakistan can only provide political support. Nevertheless, Pakistan has also become a favourite in the last few years. Is it correct to say that an anti-Indian sentiment is a major reason for igniting a pro-Pakistan trend? While the southern neighbours are aware of India's strained relations with Pakistan and that any larger role played by Pakistan in their territory would irritate India, for them Pakistan is an instrument for exercising a carrot and stick policy to keep Indian in check. Unfortunately, Pakistan's support for religious extremism has subtly endangered all the three nations. The following sections will analyse some of the threats.

Sri Lanka

Looking at the individual countries, India's relations with Sri Lanka has been historic mainly due to their geographical proximity. Both the major communities – the Sinhalese and the Tamils migrated from India at different points in history, a fact which cannot be denied. But what is not publically acknowledged is the inherent animosity of the Sinhalese towards India. The way Buddhism moved out of India was not pleasant. Religious revivalism in northern and southern India and the attack on Buddhists throughout India inflicted deep wounds on the psyche of the Sinhalese. They continue to fear that India would try, at one point or another, to annex their country, and the Sinhalese would have no other option but to jump into the sea. The assimilation of Sikkim into India, Bangladesh Liberation War of 1971 and India's subtle role in the Balochistan conflict are all seen as India's modus operandi to keep the entire region under its control. The entire ethnic conflict in Sri Lanka in a nutshell revolves around, what one calls, "the island mind-set"; the inherent fear of external interference. The Sinhalese fear of India that they see Tamils as agents of India who were sent to their island to vanquish the entire Sinhalese race. Four illustrations given below explain how Sri Lanka reacts to India.

The First incident took place in July 1983, when Amb. Shankar Bajpai was the Additional Secretary in charge of Sri Lanka and Bernard Tilakaratne was the Sri Lankan High Commissioner in New Delhi. Five days before the organized riots took place in Sri Lanka, Shankar Bajpai summoned Bernard Tilakaratne to the Foreign Office and told him "about India's concerns on what was happening in Jaffna". Bajpai made particular reference to the Emergency Regulations that were operative in Jaffna permitting disposal of the dead without inquests. The Sri Lankan envoy ventured to ask whether the "concern" was conveyed from Tamil Nadu. He was told that the concern was being expressed "at the highest political level". Understandably the Sri Lankan press reacted hysterically accusing India of "meddling with the internal affairs of Sri Lanka". "Big brother, shut up" was one of the screaming headlines in a newspaper.[2]

The second illustration is with reference to the establishment of the Sampur coal based power plant, a project supported by NTPC (National Thermal Power Corporation) India. This project was conceptualized in 2006, but took nearly 6 years to even obtain basic clearances. On February 26, 2012, Sri Lanka's Power and Energy Minister Champika Ranawaka said that the construction of the plant would commence from that year. Sri Lankan papers reacted by accusing that the "Sampur coal power project proceeded under Indian pressure". In contrast the Chinese-supported Norochcholai Power Plant was implemented in the shortest period since its conceptualization in 2007. This plant progressed to phase two and three by the end of 2014.

The third illustration is about the Comprehensive Economic Partnership Agreement (CEPA) that has been hanging in the air for more than a decade now. India and Sri Lanka signed a Free Trade Agreement in 1998. Since then the trade between the two countries have expanded multi-fold. Based on the successes and shortfalls of this agreement, India and Sri Lanka started negotiating about the CEPA in 2003. Each time there were prospects of signing the agreement, growing opposition to this agreement from powerful sections in the Sri Lankan establishment stalled the initiative. According to well-known Sri Lanka watchers, the ruling parties are encouraging these dissenting voices in order to use it as leverage against India. Many fear that this agreement would become advantage to Indian business houses against Sri Lankan businesses.

The fourth illustration is about Sri Lanka's cold approach towards India's conflict with Pakistan during the Bangladesh Liberation War of 1971. It should be impressed that in February 1971, India withdrew landing and over flying facilities to the Pakistani International Airlines (PIA). But to the shock of New Delhi, Sri Lanka in March 1971 allowed 16 east bound and 15 west bound Pakistani Air Force planes to land at Katunayake airport for refuelling. Indian defence analysts have asserted that these flights flown by plain clothed Pakistani pilots who were carrying arms and ammunitions to West Pakistan. This move by Sri Lanka comes at a time when the Indian Armed Force saved the Sri Lankan Prime Minister and the government from the JVP insurrection.[3] What is more, Sri Lanka was one of the last non-Islamic countries to recognise the liberation of Bangladesh.

Despite this cold approach by the Sri Lankan Prime Minister Mrs. Bandaranaike, the Indian Prime Minister Mrs. Gandhi handed over the island of Katchchativu to Sri Lanka in 1974 as a personal favour to the former. By this favour, Mrs. Gandhi surely showcased an instance of her deep friendship with Mrs. Bandaranaike over the betterment of the lives of fishermen in Tamil Nadu[4]. Has the transfer of this island improved India's image in Sri Lanka? The answer is a big NO. Rather, the transfer of Katchachativu to Sri Lanka has led to long drawn conflict between the Tamil fishermen of both the countries, despite belonging to one ethnicity.

Sri Lanka is a fascinating laboratory to study not only the ethnic question, but also the handling of the fishermen issue. It is a widely known fact that over the centuries, fishermen have been fishing in all areas where plenty of fish is available and no maritime borders stop their movement. Sri Lankan fishermen enter Indian and Maldivian waters, Indian fishermen enter Sri Lankan and Pakistani waters, Bangladeshis enter Myanmar, and the Japanese and Taiwanese trawlers cover all of Asia's waters. The maritime boundaries are restrictions imposed by the State which have led to the development of strains in bilateral relations, loss of human lives and destruction of fishing crafts.[5]

An interesting fact about the India-Sri Lanka fishing issue is that it is not only Indian Tamil fishermen who cross maritime boundaries and enter Sri Lankan territory, even the Sinhalese fishermen cross boundaries to reach the Andaman and Nicobar Islands and Lakshadweep islands. This is not a new phenomenon and has been going on for years. While reports of Indian fishermen going into Sri Lankan waters have become major news, it is not with the Sinhalese infiltration in Indian waters. The issue of fishermen being killed and arrested has been in the media since 2002, when the Ceasefire Agreement (CFA) was signed between the Sri Lankan Government and the (Liberation Tigers of Tamil Eelam) LTTE. The CFA paved the way for the removal of restrictions against the Sri Lankan fishermen for fishing in the Northern Province. Until this period, the Indian fishermen had unrestricted access to the northern waters of Sri Lanka. It is hard not to say that there were no aberrations between the fishermen of both countries[6]. What is more important is that over the years, both the fishing groups have agreed to share and cooperate with each other, and the only concern the Sri Lankan fishermen raised was regarding the bottom trawlers used by the Indian fishermen. This crisis continues even at this juncture, but in the last few years scenarios have changed. While the fishermen have been more sympathetic, the Sri Lankan Navy has been ruthless in their approach. Capture of Indian fishing vessels and fishermen have become the norm of the day.

The fishermen issue between India and Sri Lanka is not only an example of conflict between the two countries but also provides opportunities for interaction and working together. Sadly, it also becomes an instance of lost opportunities. On October 26, 2008 the two sides reached an elaborate understanding to put in place "practical arrangements to deal with bona fide Indian and Sri Lankan fishermen crossing the international maritime boundary line".[7] This arrangement was also the first official acknowledgement of the fact that fishermen crossed boundaries. This also called for an arrangement wherein this region was to be treated as common heritage rather than being considered as contested territory. But sadly, both the governments of India and Sri Lanka did not show any interest in formalising this agreement. Hence, yet another chance at cooperation was lost.

While India - Sri Lanka relations is about missed opportunities, India - Maldives relations is not only about missed opportunities but also has to do with New Delhi's total indifference in its approach.

Maldives

While, Sri Lanka has all the reasons to fear India due to its geographical proximity, Maldives has very little to fear considering its viability for India. Straddling the Indian Ocean across the equator, Maldives is one of the most sparsely populated and, at the same time, geographically dispersed countries in the world. Despite its geographical location in the Indian Ocean, which is quite vital for India, it has always been ignored by New Delhi. We have ignored it to such an extent that Maldives is slowly turning out to be a threat to India's security, more so because in recent months, internal developments have taken a turbulent turn with an assertive President, active opposition, a weak judiciary, and general lawlessness.

Maldives not being able to receive New Delhi's attention is not new. Ever since Gayoom took over as the President of Maldives in 1978, he has remained a blue eyed boy of the South Block in New Delhi. During his tenure, India was involved in the Maldivian affairs only twice. 'Op Cactus' and 'Op Rainbow' are the two major operations India has had in Maldives.

Op Cactus was in November 1988, when President Gayoom was threatened by a coup staged by around 200 Sri Lankan Tamil mercenaries of the PLOTE (People's Liberation Organization of Tamil Eelam) of Sri Lanka, who had gone at the behest of a Maldivian businessman, Abdullah Luthufee who was residing in Sri Lanka, and the Maldivian National Security Service. The timely intervention of the Indian armed forces within 24 hours was instrumental in stalling the coup and flushing out the mercenaries. Earlier in 1980, there had been a failed coup attempt orchestrated by the British. Op Rainbow was for tsunami relief, a purely humanitarian venture. India also gave two fast attack crafts to Maldives in April, 2006 during the visit of the Indian defence minister to Maldives. These are the Trinkat Class Fast Attack Craft and INS Tillanchang, a 260-ton Fast-Attack craft.

Although Maldives obtained its freedom from the British in 1965, its independent foreign policy came into existence only after the British vacated the Gan Islands in 1976. Close geographical proximity with Diego Garcia makes Maldivian security and independence extremely important for India and other regional actors. The US did make an attempt to take over the Gan islands following UK's exit from Maldives in 1968, but requested the use of some of the island's resorts for recreation purposes for its soldiers posted in Diego Garcia, but this request was turned down in view of India's pressure.

With regard to India - Maldives relations, apart from the traditional historical links, formal relations can be traced to Maldives' declaration of independence in November 1965 and India was the third country to recognise Maldives. The first state level visit was in 1974 when Prime Minister Mr Ahmed Zaki of Maldives made an official visit to India. Since then, there have been frequent bilateral visits by the leaders of both countries. Most of these visits are important to Maldives because with every visit, Maldives has benefited economically.

Bilateral trade with Maldives is weighed deeply in favour of India. We are the third largest exporter to Maldives. India and Maldives trade relations currently stand at Rs.700 crores. The Indian community is the second largest expatriate community numbering nearly 26,000, consisting of doctors, nurses, technicians, teachers, labourers.

The cordial relations that began during Gayoom's period continued even during President Nasheed's tenure until 2012. Having been elected democratically as President of Maldives, the Indian scholars on Maldives feared that President Nasheed might go closer to China and western countries, and against the interest of the Government of India. This was because during the democratic struggle that started in August 2004, New Delhi had been totally indifferent to the Maldivian Democratic Party (MDP) led by Nasheed. On many occasions New Delhi did not recognise Nasheed's contribution to the democratisation of Maldives. The Government of India in order to please Gayoom, denied audience to Nasheed and his team every time they visited New Delhi. It was only in 2008 that New Delhi opened its doors to the MDP. By this time, Nasheed had already been recognised as opposition leader and Presidential candidate. The author of this paper accompanied the visiting MDP delegation from Chennai to New Delhi. The way the Indian government treated the delegation led by Nasheed was appalling. Nasheed and his delegation were forced to stand along with the common man in a long line for security check at the airport during their travel from Chennai. On the contrary, the week following the MDP delegation's visit to New Delhi, the then President Gayoom, sent his family members to New Delhi to apprise the situation in Maldives, and this delegation was received with full honours.

Despite this treatment meted out to Nasheed, on becoming the President of Maldives, he proved to be a good friend to the Government of India. It should be emphasised that President Gayoom, during his long thirty year tenure, tried to use external actors like, the UK, the US, China and Pakistan as a check to the growing Indian influence in this region. During the 1988 coup staged by the Sri Lankan Tamil mercenaries, President Gayoom had first sought support from the UK, Malaysia, Singapore, the US, Pakistan, Sri Lanka. With hardly any support from other countries he was advised to seek India's help. This was never a concern during President Nasheed's tenure. India was offered the Gan Islands, which is in the southern region of Maldives, for its restoration and use of the Indian Navy for monitoring the Indian Ocean. In addition to this, the Maldivian airport contract was also given to India for modernisation. Time and again, President Nasheed ensured India that it was given the first priority. But sadly, the political crisis that ensued after 2012 not only had a deep impact on Maldives but also on its relations with India.

Initially India did not show any interest in the political crisis in Maldives, but the Presidential coup of 2012 had made India party to the crisis. Since then, India-Maldives relations has gone into a nose dive. Though the February 7, 2012 uprising and *coup d' etat,* which overthrew President Nasheed's government came as a surprise to the world, it had its roots in the growing fundamentalism which had been brewing for over a decade. President Gayoom's intentions of becoming the President of Maldives again added to the crisis. The international community including India was aware of the ensuing crisis for years but had hardly showed any interest in resolving this issue.

The biggest challenge in India – Maldives relations came about when President Nasheed took refuge in the Indian High Commission premises at Male on 13th February 2012 for 11 days following an arrest warrant issued by the Hulhulumale Magistrate court to bring him before the court by 4.30 pm. The Indian Government until then was only raising concerns about the political uprising in Maldives, but with President Nasheed seeking refuge, India became an unwilling party to the crisis. The Maldivian national media, supporters of Gayoom and the then incumbent President Waheed openly spoke against India saying that 'India was showing big brother attitude against smaller countries in South Asia'. Reacting to Indian involvement, the Indian conglomerate GMR, which was involved in the modernisation of Ibrahim Nassir International Airport, was thrown out unceremoniously in 2012. The incumbent President Abdulla Yameen, has also been keen on keeping India at bay, considering that he has been, in recent months, asserting his autocratic rule and has ruthlessly been working against any form of democratic governance. The biggest worry among these developments is the rapid spread of religious fundamentalism.

Democracy in Maldives has become a total sham, the country that was moderate and modern is now a hot bed of Wahhabi activism. The following illustrations explain the growth of fundamentalism in Maldives.

First, on September 29th 2007, a bomb blast rocked a recreation park injuring eight Chinese and two Japanese; two British tourists were also injured. Following the bomb blast, the standoff between the Maldivian Security Forces and the masked men at the Himandhoo Island of the Alif Alif Atoll who were protecting the mastermind of the bomb blast was a clear sign of the presence of Wahhabi elements in Maldives and their role in the bomb blast in Male.

Second, the religious conservatives have become increasingly aggressive in the recent years. The government's efforts to revise the penal code came under intense opposition from vocal sections that want sharia law punishments like death penalty, flogging and amputations to be included in the rulings. Several public demonstrations supporting flogging have taken place in Male in the recent years and those who have spoken against it have been threatened.

Third, there is also an increasing danger of Maldivians who go to other Islamic countries for their education. Reports of connections between Maldivians and fundamentalists groups were available as early as 2002, when 28-year-old Ibrahim Fauzee, a Maldivian national, was arrested in Karachi and was taken to Guantanamo Bay by the US security forces for his connections with Al Qaeda. There was an announcement by the Maldivian Defence Ministry about the arrest of nine armed Maldivians in the northern district of Pakistan on April 2, 2009. There were also reports of arrest of three Maldivians in the first week of March 2009. These Maldivians were allegedly on their way to join the Taliban or were planning an attack. One of those arrested, Saeed Ahmed, is said to be an accused in the Sultan Park explosion case but was said to have been released earlier for want of evidence. It should be emphasised that some of the Maldivians who were trained by the LeT and the Taliban, and arrested in Kerala were working towards setting up their centres in Kerala and Tamil Nadu.

Fourth, the decision to permit religious group Tablighi Jamaat to preach in Maldives has caused controversy, with some members of the public walking out of mosques in protest. The Adaalath Party has defended this groups members visiting Maldives. Despite concerns raised by moderate sections of the society, the government has allowed members of Tablighi Jamaat to speak at various mosques. There are fears that fundamentalism has gained enough ground in the peripheral areas of Maldives.[8]It may not be a surprise if the entire population of Maldives starts following Wahhabism in the coming years.

Conclusion

Sub-regional relations between India-Sri Lanka, and Maldives has always been asymmetrical mainly due to the geography and the demography of these countries. Sri Lanka and Maldives fear that any cooperation with

India would only lead to the big brother taking an upper hand and not an equal partnership. In fact, there is a strong accusation that SAARC could become a shark association, wherein India might swallow its smaller neighbours instead of supporting their growth. It is this fear that leads all the Indian neighbours to look for external support.

So what should India do? It will be to the benefit of India if we handle our neighbours using the carrot and stick policy. Being checkmated by our neighbours with the support of external actors is definitely better than ignoring them and leading ourselves to a crisis. The growth of Jihadi fundamentalism in our backyard is a typical example of this. In 2004, Late Mr. Raman, a leading strategic thinker warned India: "The threat to us from Pakistan through Sri Lanka is more tactical than strategic, more subversive than military, more political than economic. China is a dragon, but Pakistan is still only a pinprick. We should be alert to the possibility of China and Pakistan acting in tandem in Sri Lanka and Maldives to undermine the Indian influence, but there is as yet no evidence of this possibility becoming a reality, but it could in the long-term. Our policy response should nip this bud before it starts blooming."

It took us nearly 10 years to realise that this threat was becoming a reality. In 2014, New Delhi for the first time acknowledged that Jihadi threat to India is likely to come from our southern neighbours than from Pakistan. It is still a surprise that India has ignored the growing religious fundamentalism in our backyard until now. To quote Dr. Chandrasekharan, Director, South Asian Analysis Group,[9]

"Then, of course, to go back to the growing Islamic fundamentalism. I have seen Male since 1989 and in my three visits there, the Male I saw in 1989, in 1991 and now is completely different. I see more of the trappings of the fundamentalism. Almost 50 per cent of the women seem to be wearing the Muga, as they call the burqa in the local language, a certain amount of conservatism creeping in. [10]

It is time India seriously looked into confidence building measures with Sri Lanka and Maldives. The new government in Sri Lanka is likely to be more pro-India. India needs to use this chance to provide them with better support for reconstruction of the war affected regions. The international community including the diaspora have shown interest in the development of Northern and Eastern Sri Lanka. As a step forward, the Sri Lankan Government has lifted its ban on the daispora groups so that they can visit or return to the island. It is important that India should join this bandwagon and not miss this opportunity. With regard to Maldives, India needs to stand by the democratic forces, as the more New Delhi support an autocratic regime; it is more likely that they will become a failed country like Pakistan. While non-interference into others internal affairs is important, India should firmly impress on our southern neighbours that any anti-Indian activity in their territory would not be tolerated.

Two important areas in which India can support the neighbouring states are education and health care. Both Sri Lankans and Maldivians continue to look forward to visiting India for higher education and also for health care, as they have few options in their countries. Until now, the Indian involvement in education of the youth has been negligible. All that India has established is a training institute in Maldives and we also offer very few scholarships for students from Maldives to study in India. In Sri Lanka, India can invest and also concentrate in supporting the advancement of educational sector. While providing more scholarships for students sounds lucrative, it will not be a viable solution in the long run. If only India based premier educational institutions and invested in the education sector in the southern neighbours, there would hardly be any youth who go to countries like Pakistan and Saudi Arabia for higher education and be influenced by Wahhabism.

Health care systems also continue to be in poor state. It is well known that Maldivians and Sri Lankans continue to travel to Kerala, Tamil Nadu and Karnataka for treatment. Sadly until now, Indian support in health care is not up to desired levels. The need of the hour is not only to invest in health care, but also subsidise medical facilities to both Maldivians and Sri Lankans who come for treatment to India. One cannot deny the issues in the asymmetrical relations between India – Sri Lanka and Maldives, however, if India is able to concentrate more on the southern neighbours without bullying them, both these countries would be great partners in supporting India's security.

Endnotes

1   Peter M Hall, "Asymmetric Relationships and Processes of power", in Harvey A. Farberman, *Foundations of Interpretive Sociology: Original Essays in Symbolic Interaction,* (Greenwich: Jai Press, 1985).

2   V. Suryanarayan and Ashik Bonofer, "India should revise its stance on HR violations by Colombo", *The Sri Lanka Guardian,* available at http://www.srilankaguardian.org/2011/09/india-should-revise-its-atance-on-hr.html   as on October 1, 2015.

3   Sankaran Krishna, "Postcolonial Insecurities: India, Sri Lanka, and the Question of Nationhood," (Minneapolis: University of Minnesota Press, 1999), p.259

4   Neil Devotta, "When Individuals, States, and Systems Collide, India's Foreign Policy towards Sri Lanka", ed, Sumit Ganguly, *India's Foreign Policy, Retrospect and Prospect,* (NewDelhi: Oxford University Press, 2013), p.41

5   Prof. V. Suryanarayan and R. Swaminathan, "Contested Territory or Common Heritage?" *Thinking Out of The Box,* (Chennai: Ganesh & Co, 2009), p.7

6   During 2003 and 2004, there have been number of incidents of Indian boats being captured by Sri Lankan fishermen and handed over to the authorities for further action. In some instances there have been clashes at sea between the two sides and in 2004, a Sri Lankan fisherman was killed in one such clash.

7   Gurnam Chand, "Fishermen Issue between India and Sri Lanka", *Mainstream,* Vol. XLIX, No 13 available at http://www.mainstreamweekly.net/article2634.html as on 10 October 2015.

8   Ibrahim Mohamed, Religious group causes divide among scholars, *Minivan News,* available at http://minivannewsarchive.com/ as on October 15, 2015

9   Dr. Chandrasaker expressed his fears during an interaction at the Chennai Chapter of the Observer Research Foundation.

10 Adding to this comment Dr. Chandrasakerin an article published in South Asia Analysis Group also wrote that "The Deputy Secretary General of the MDP only said that I was not necessary to wear the burqa and she was forced to resign from the party post and has been asked to explain. She has been given an ultimatum: either she apologizes or she resigns from the official party post of being a Deputy Secretary General of the party. She chose to resign from the party. There are visits of the preachers coming and the question is, the

problem is how to stop it with the modern methods of the Internet, the e mail and such things, this is an issue that has problems which most of the time is preoccupying. I must appreciate President Gayoom for being able to keep the Islamic extremism at bay, particularly the Wahabbi type. It is hundred percent Sunni Islamic country and this is another issue because practically they cannot maintain a hundred percent Sunni Islam character because with the increase in globalisation, there is bound to be inter-religious liaisons and inter-cultural connections, in form of marriages and so on there needs to be some provisions for peaceful cohabitation of other religions."

Chapter 3

India, Sri Lanka and Maldives: Shared Commonality yet Challenges to Sub-regional Cooperation

M. Mayilvaganan

Introduction

Sri Lanka and Maldives are the maritime bordering neighbours who share intimate historical, cultural, religious, ethnic and linguistic interaction with India. All the communities in these island nations are in one or other way considered being from India in every sense, as the geographical proximity, cultural and religious linkages propose. Nonetheless, this proximity had played a part in forcing them—Sri Lankans and Maldivians—to exhibit that they are 'distinct' from India. The ruling elites desire to shed away their 'Indian-ness' as an effort to defend and promote their own 'identity' which is essential for their existence. For instance, the majority ruling Sinhalese in Sri Lanka, desire to be recognized as an ethnic group with a distinctive identity, which is notably superior from that of the Sri Lankan Tamils and the Muslims. The 'identity' of being distinct has indeed contributed to distrust in their relationship with India and which in turn challenges the sub-regional cooperation in the region.

India's size, growing economy and military power has unavoidably scared Sri Lankan and Maldivian elites who consequently tried to balance 'mighty' India in the form of seeking external strategic cooperation with countries like China. This hedging by Colombo and Malé has fostered distrust between India from time to time. India's interest in the affairs of these island nations are intertwined with New Delhi's strategic and security interest in the region, Indian Ocean Region in general which in turn had a bearing on elusive sub-regional cooperation.

The paper intends to discuss the challenges of sub-regional cooperation in South Asia comprising of India, Sri Lanka and Maldives despite the clear cultural, religious, ethnic and linguistic interaction between them. The main thrust of this paper is the power asymmetry; desire for 'distinct' identity coupled with geographical proximity has inherently prompted smaller states like Sri Lanka and Maldives in the region to evade sub-regional cooperation with India or in building robust bilateral relationship.

India-Sri Lanka Linkages

The culture, religion, language, society, arts and even food habits of Sri Lanka have been profoundly influenced by India. Sinhalese, Tamils, and Muslims of Sri Lanka share common cultural attributes.

Buddhism Links

Geographically, India and Sri Lanka is separated by a narrow stretch of water known as Palk Strait. The distance between two countries is nearly 22 miles (23 km). Apparently, for ages the only significant foreign impact that Sri Lanka had was from India. The bonds between two countries are evident from anthropology, linguistic, cultural, archaeology, DNA samples, etc. The Sinhalese, accounting for about 73.8% of the total population are the descendants from India. They are said to be immigrants from the Bengal-Odisha region[1], what is earlier known as Kalinga region in the eastern coast of India. However, some contend that they are from Gujarat. Whatever may be, the reality is that they are from India[2].

Buddhism is a main source of religion and culture for a majority of its people (Sinhalese). The religion, Buddhism, which originated in India was brought across to Sri Lanka in the 3rd century BCE by Arahat Mahinda (Prince Mahendra), the son of Emperor Asoka. As an emissary Mahinda introduced Buddhism to Anuradhapura monarch some 2300 years ago. He also founded the order of monks in Sri Lanka[3]. His sister Sanghamitra or Sanghamitta Theri followed him to Sri Lanka who founded the order of Buddhist nuns there. The arrival of Mahinda in the 3rd century BCE.

is recorded in the Sri Lanka's Great Chronicle, the Mahavamsa, and substantiated by a rock inscription found in Amparai. Incidentally, the Sri Maha Bo tree in Anuradhapura and the Sacred Tooth, a relic of Lord Buddha in Kandy (gifted by King Guhaseeva) are well known gifts from India that portrays India's connection even today[4]. Notably for majority of Sri Lankans—Sinhalese—India remains a major place for pilgrimage. Buddha Gaya and other religious places like Tirupati tops Sinhalese visit. In fact, Buddhism laid the foundation for India-Sri Lanka ties since ages. The exposition of Sacred Kapilavastu Relics (fragments of Buddha's bones) in Sri Lanka by India in 1978 and 2012 is one more testimony of the Buddhist links[5].

Interestingly Tamil Nadu, the closest South Indian state and Sri Lanka who are diagonally opposite today shared trade and Buddhist linkages since the early years of the Christian era and the 14th century. Indeed, some have argued that Buddhism may have gone to Sri Lanka from Tamil Nadu, contrary to the general impression that it went from Bengal or Odisha region. Mahinda, the son of emperor Ashoka, may have introduced Buddhism in Tamil Nadu before embarking to Sri Lanka. The Brahmi inscriptions in caves in Thirunelveli and Madurai districts exemplify that Buddhism came to Tamil Nadu as early as 3rd century BCE. Besides, the Tamil literatures like "Manimekalai' talks about the interaction between the monks in Tamil Nadu and Sri Lanka[6]. Particularly, there is mention about the presence of monks of Sri Lanka in Vanchi (present day Karur), which was the capital of the Chera Kings of Tamil Nadu. Similarly, Mahavamsa, the great epic of Sri Lanka mentions about the exodus of monks from Sri Lanka—when Kalinga Magha (from Odisha established a Kingdom in Rajarata) persecuted Buddhists in the early 13th century—who found shelter in South Indian kingdom's "Pandya" and "Cholas."[7]

Besides, evidently the spread and growth of Buddhism in Sri Lanka had much to do with fruitful contacts with Buddhist centres of learning in South India such as Kaveripumpattinam (Poompuhar), Kanchipuram and Madurai with Anuradhapura, Amparai etc. in Sri Lanka. The Buddhist monasteries, monks and scholars in India and Sri Lanka shared close ties. For instance, South Indian monks like Buddhadutta (from Uraiyur), Dhammapala, Vajrabodhi and Buddhaghosha were credited for the advancement of Buddhism in Sri Lanka, specifically from the 5th century to 7 century AD. Buddhadutta, a great Buddhism scholar, was credited with authoring Maduratta Vilasini (commentary on the Buddhavamsa, which is a compilation of legends dealing with the lives of Gotama) and the Jinalankara[8]. Significantly, King Parakramabahu II has been told to gain the religious texts from India to revive Buddhism in Sri Lanka.

Language connection

The Pali text, Sinhala language and literatures are more proof of the strong linkages between India and Sri Lanka. The Sinhala, language of majority Sinhalese, has connection with Indian languages. The majority Buddhist Sinhalese, who speaks Sinhala, is associated with the North Indian Prakit,[9] a branch of the Indo-European language family and a descendant of the ancient Indian Brahmi script. In fact, Buddhism is the fountainhead of Sinhalese literature. Pali texts that were brought by Arahat Mahinda were translated into Sinhala which were again translated back into Pali by Rev. Buddhagosha, who came from India in the 5th century. According to the literature, when the Sinhala texts were destroyed in Sri Lanka, Pali became the sacred language of Buddhism. The earliest existing chronicle works of importance such as Dharmasena Thera's 13th century Saddharma Ratnavaliya and Saddharmalankaraya (1398-1410) by Dharmakirthi TheraII, are indeed based on earlier Pali texts. The great epics of Sri Lanka; Mahavamsa and Culavamsa were written in Pali text.[10]

King Sena's Siyabaslakara, a rough translation of Dandin's earlier Sanskrit work Kavyadarsha in the 9th century, and Kalidasa's Mega Dutha inspired Sinhalese sandesa. Message poems such as the Mayura Sandesaya (the Peacock Messenger Poem) and the Tisara Sandesaya (the Swan Messenger Poem) are the existing evidence of literature links between India and Sri Lanka. In addition, the similarities between Sinhala and Hindi are evident from the following words such as karnaa (Hindi) and karanaa (Sinhala) means "to do"; dekhnaa (Hindi) and dakinaa (Sinhala) means "to see."

The minority Sri Lankan Tamils and their ethnic counterpart Indian Tamils or Plantation Tamils who speak Tamil, a language of the Dravidian family, comprise 18.5% of the total population. Another minority Sri Lankan Muslims who largely speak Tamil account for 7.2% of the total population. The Tamil language has contributed for robust bonds between Tamils in India and Tamils in Sri Lanka. Also the linguistic heritage of the

Sri Lankan Muslims includes words from Tamil and Malayalam apart from Persian, one of the key to the extraordinary links with India.

Hinduism Connection

Equally, Hinduism, another Indian religion too had a significant influence on Sri Lanka. Apart from minority Tamils who were predominantly Hindus, the majority Sinhalese too had come under the potent influence of Hinduism and Hindu rituals.[11] The presence of God Vishnu, God Skanda, Goddess Pattini and God Saman, four popular cardinal guardian gods of Sinhalese or say, Sri Lanka is the living proof. The images of these Hindu Gods occupy a prominent place in Buddhist Viharas. God Vishnu is worshipped as "Upulvan" (Blue-Lotus-Colored), and is considered as the Kshetra-Pāla (Protector of the Land). God Skanda (Murugan or Karthikeyan by Hindus) is believed as the protector of the individual. God Saman (is identified with Lakshman) and Goddess Pattini by the Sinhalese Buddhists and Kannaki Amman by the Sri Lankan Tamil Hindu along other Hindu deities such as Ganesha, Saraswathi, Kali and Ayyanayake (Aiyyanar to the Tamils) finds prominent places in Sri Lanka and are worshipped by the majority Sinhalese.

The kavadiattam or penance dancing rituals which are a common feature of religious Hindu rituals in South India is followed in southern Sri Lanka Skanda temple Katirgama, holiest shrine to Buddhists in Sri Lanka[12]. Also the prominence of Nekath, the auspicious time in Buddhist weddings like the Hindus too is an instance of the Indian connection.

The Chola's patronage of ancient Tamil Saivate temples such as Koneswaram (Trincomalee), Thiruketheeswaram (Mannar), Munnesvaram (Puttalam) and Tirukkovil (Ampara District) which are evident from the stone inscriptions portrays India's bond with Sri Lanka.[13] The Shiva Dewalaya in Polonnaruwa of the 11th century, Nalanda Gedige of Matale of 8-10th century, and Kataragama temple are attestation of Hinduism linkages. Likewise, the Tamil inscription of Paràkramabâhu at the Hindu temple of Munnesvaram in Sri Lanka records the grant of land and money by the king to that temple and its Brahmins. The use of Sanskrit and Tamil languages in this and several other records testifies the Indian connection in the island nation.[14]

The Indian literature like Ramayana divulge about the connection between India and Sri Lanka. The presence of places such as SitaEliya, Ussangoda, Koneswaram etc. in Sri Lanka that are mentioned in the epic are further testimony of the association. In the same way, Silapathikaram, Tamil literature mentions about Gajabahu I, the Sinhalese king's presence at the consecration of a temple to Kannagi by the Chera king Senguttuvan.

Archeological and Maritime Links

The archaeological findings, explorations and excavations at various sites in India and Sri Lanka part from epigraphical and numismatic evidences of different periods, and literary records, provides maritime trade and cultural links between India and Sri Lanka. The finding of Rouletted Ware from Anuradhapura and Jaffna in Sri Lanka indicates that it might have come from Arikamedu or some other sites of South India[15]. The excavation of Punch Marked Coins (PMC) and the Northern Black Polished (NBP) ware considered to be originally from the Gangetic valley at Gedige and Anuradhapura in Sri Lanka illustrate the contact of Orissa with Sri Lanka. Similarly, finding of coin of King Sahasamalla, Medival Kandyan King, dating from the 11th or 12th century AD at Manikpatna (eastern Odisha) is a testimony of Indian-Sri Lanka ties.[16]

Maurya's, Kalinga's, and Chola's of India had trade ties with Sri Lanka. The evidence: different pottery found at ports, trade centres and hinterland sites—from Manikapatna (Odisha), Poompuhar, Arikamedu, Sopatma (Tamil Nadu and Pondicherry), and Masulipatnam (Andhra Pradesh). All these suggest the widespread overseas trade between India and Sri Lanka.

Royal Links

The regular links between royal families of India and Sri Lanka is apparent from the martial alliance.[17] In fact, the first Sinhala King Vijaya (544 BC) reportedly married a Pandyan Princess from Madurai. And similarly Telugu Satavahana dynasty's 17th monarch Hāla (20-24 CE) married a princess from Sri Lanka. The marital alliances between Kandyan kings of Sri Lanka and Nayak princesses from Madurai and Thanjavur of India for decades were last available substantiation. Sri Wickrama Rajasinghe (Prince Kannasamy), Tamil Nayakkar king of Kandy and the last Kandyan king was the relative of Nayaka kings of Madurai and Tanjavur.[18] In fact, he was a royal prisoner by the British to Vellore who died in January 30, 1832 at Vellore, India. Earlier, incidentally, when a Sinhalese Kandyan king, NarendraSinha, died without an offspring, the brother of his Madurai Nayak queen succeeded the throne in 1739 under the coronated name of Sri Vijaya Raja Sinha. In addition, Sapumal Kumara, the adopted son and general of Parakramabahu VI, was said to be the son of a Kerala warrior married to a local Sri Lankan woman from a family of rank. Also royal families of Gampola and Kotte were reportedly having a marital alliance with the Kerala rulers of India.

Incidentally, even the genetic studies indicate that both Tamils and Sinhalese clusters in Sri Lanka were affiliated with the population of the Indian subcontinent.[19]

Islam Connection

Marakayar of Tamil Nadu, Mappila Muslims of Kerala traditionally had links with Sri Lankan Muslims[20]. Kayalpatnam, Kulasekarapatnam, Kilakarai, Maricarpatnam, Adirampatnam, Tondi, Karaikal etc., along the Tamil Nadu coast; Kottakal, Kochi of Malabar along the Kerala coast and the southern seacoast of Ceylon like Galle, Batticola are the major centre of Muslim trade and the congregation of the Indian and Sri Lankan Muslims. Even today there are close cultural systems between the Muslims of Sri Lanka and Tamil Nadu. Muslim missionaries from India, particularly Tamil Nadu have throughout the ages influenced Sri Lanka and helped shape the religious thinking of the Muslims of Sri Lanka.

Indian Leaders Influence

The Indian Independence movement and the Indian leaders had an influence on Sri Lanka and their Independence movement. Delegates from Sri Lanka such as S.W.R.D. Bandaranaike addressed sessions in India, while delegates from India such as Gandhi and Nehru addressed sessions at Sri Lanka during 1930's and 1940's. Sri Palee College in Horana, Sri Lanka, was inspired by Tagore's model of education at the Vishva-Bharati University in Shantiniketan that was inaugurated by Tagore in 1934. Concept of Satyagraha by Gandhi was transplanted in Sri Lanka by Sarvodaya Shramadana Movement founded by Dr A. T. Ariyaratne in

1958. Equally EVR Periyar & Dravidian movement of Tamil Nadu, India had considerable influence on Tamil movements and politics in Sri Lanka.

Even today, Bollywood and South Indian films are still influential in Sri Lanka. Many Indian teledramas are dubbed in Sinhala and Hindi songs are played in public and on local television channels. The profound influence of India on Sri Lanka is evident in every sphere—religion, culture, economic, political, etc. In short, although Sri Lanka and India are two distinct countries in the region, they are connected by shared history, religion, language, morals, and culture.

Maldives: The Indian Connection

Anthropology and Language Links

The Maldivians were identified as mainly Indo-Aryan line from the anthropological point of view. Research suggests that they may be the migrant from the regions of Kerala, Karnataka, Tamil Nadu and Sri Lanka. Even Dhivehi language, the official language of Maldives is categorized as of Indo-Iranian Sanskrit origin.[21] Notably, it is said to be derived from ancient and medieval Maharashtri Prakrit and considered as closely related to Marathi, Konkani and Sinhalese languages. The influence of the old Tulu language from the Karnataka region is noticeable. Incidentally, it is also the first language in Minicoy in the Union territory of Lakshadweep, India, where the Mahl dialect of the Maldivian language is spoken.

The great Maldivian epic Koimala, reports the arrival of a protagonist from India/ Sri Lanka, bringing with him his royal lineage, who landed on a northern atoll, and then made Male his capital.[22] Interestingly, the name *koi* is said to be from Malayalam *koya*, son of the prince, which is also the name of a high caste group in the Lakshadvweep Islands. These ancient literatures record points to India's connection to the island nations.

Religion & Cultural Similarities

The research studies suggest that before the arrival of Islam in 12th century, Buddhism was the prominent religion of Maldives. The works of scholars like H.C.P. Bell (1922) and others, documents the evidence of several remains of Buddhist stupas, with coins, inscriptions, and various artefacts including finding of statue of Goddess Tara in the Maldivian atolls.[23]

The Maldivian culture is categorised into three main layers, namely Tamil-Malayalam substratum with its many subtle roots, old Sinhala culture and language, which is the dominant element, and the phase of Arabic Influence. The Mappila Muslims of Kerala and Marakayar of Tamil Nadu are considered to be the earliest Muslims from India who had close links with the Maldivians. In many ways the culture of the Maldives is regarded as come from a number of sources including the most important from India. Arrakal Royal Family of Cannanore (Kerala) reportedly had links and influence on Maldives.[24] It is clear that India had its share of influence on Maldives and continues to be a factor in Maldivian lives.

Challenges to Sub-Regional Cooperation

Geographical proximity, power relations, religion, trade and cultural characteristics aided ties between India, Sri Lanka and Maldives for centuries. Three countries share many common historical, spiritual and cultural attributes. The question is what affects regional or sub-regional cooperation among them?

The first and foremost is that both Sri Lanka and Maldives are looking at the present through the prism of the past in a distorted way— the falsification of history. The historical animosity and the invasion of ancient kingdoms of South India against Sri Lanka and Maldives, namely Cholas against Mahinda and the Kerala's Arakkal family against Maldives Sultan of the Maldives Hasan 'Izzud-din were kept alive by the elites in these island nations to aid their nationalist approach and in pleasing the majority. They invoked the past historical characters of their land who fought against few Indian kings in order to substantiate that they are under threat from the mighty India and thus it is important for them to establish their unique identity. In this process they try to shed their Indian-ness—the Indian connection. The arguments such as 'Aryan' Sinhalese vs. 'Dravidian' Tamils and Hinduism vs. Buddhism in Sri Lanka, and Buddhism vs. Islam in Maldives, are some of the well known 'engineered' concept that was advocated by the ruling elites in support of falsification efforts. As a result, instead of rejoicing their rich Indian links and going for the substantial regional cooperation the ruling elites have created mass hysteria against

India, which sowed seed in the minds of the people of these island nations that India is 'threat' to them—culturally, politically and militarily

The India's support to the minority Tamils in Sri Lanka since 1980s has partly contributed for this Sinhalese 'hysteria' against India. The reported statement of the Sri Lanka High Commissioner to India, Prasad Kariyawasam, dated March 27, 2013 that "today, India seems to be concerned only about the 12 per cent Tamil population in Sri Lanka who share ethnic links with Tamil Nadu. But Sinhalese too has similar but ancient links with Odisha and north India,"[25] have been forgotten is a case in point. Apparently, the internal conflict or internal politics between minority Tamils and majority Sinhalese have contributed for Sinhalese hard line approach against India. Similarly, the Mohamed Nasheed vs Abdul Gayoom domestic politics in Maldives and the former's good relations with New Delhi have cast shadow in India-Maldives ties. In summary, it can be concluded that the smaller island nations—Sri Lanka and Maldives—said apprehension against India is partly a product of their internal politics and their quest for 'distinct identity' to keep the nationalist fervour intact.

The geographical proximity in many instances serves as a blessing for nations to boost their ties with neighbours and benefit from the big ones. However, the same geographical proximity of being close to the big ones like India—in terms of size, economic and military power—have infused 'fear' in smaller Sri Lanka and Maldives. They perceive India as 'Big Brother', 'Regional Hegemony' etc. The issue of Indian fishermen poaching in the Palk Strait, the Indian Tamils support to Sri Lankan Tamils etc., have played its part in aiding anti-India sentiments within Sri Lankan. With the escalation of the crisis internally, Sri Lanka and Maldives have increasingly adopted an approach diverging strongly from that of their Indian neighbour.

In addition the economic concern and the perceived competition in tea, fish, etc. have complicated the pattern of economic relations. For instance, commodities such as tea and fish accounts for about two-thirds of Sri Lanka's total exports, the major source of economic sustenance of the island nation. But with the issue of Indian fishermen fishing in Sri Lankan waters, Sri Lanka is of opinion that it harms their foreign earnings. Ideologies, values and interests based on some degree of cultural and economic commonality should make it trouble-free and not as an obstacle in bringing cooperation in South Asia comprising Maldives, Sri Lanka and India.

Even though sub-regional cooperation between South Indian states—Tamil Nadu, Kerala, Karnataka, Sri Lanka and Maldives contribute for the emancipation of some of the regions from underdevelopment to economic development. Through which it may complementarities regions of these different countries to gain a comparative edge in production and export of their products.

Conclusion

A new framework for sub regional cooperation is needed based on mutual understanding and trust. For which domestically the 'chauvinists' among the Sinhalese and the Tamils in Sri Lanka should stop projecting the two communities as antagonistic entities against each other and in turn should see India as their own friendly neighbor who has its own links with each group in the island nation. Similarly the political parties in the Maldives should shed their own rivalry and linking others with India for everything. Greater cooperation among the southern states with neighboring Sri Lanka and Maldives can bring not only economic development but also increased connectivity between the people which may contribute for building trust and confidence.

The examples of "Southern Growth Triangle" (SIJORI), encompassing Singapore, Johor in Malaysia and the Indonesian island of Batam in Riau province that helped to mitigate the territorial dispute between the three countries and the cooperation among the provinces in Myanmar, Thailand and China bordering each other forming Greater Mekong Subregion ought be the exemplar for developing and cooperating among Sri Lanka, Maldives and India. This becomes more essential when the economic interaction between South India, Sri Lanka and Maldives is very minimal. Thus, trade, investment and connectivity between the three needs to be enhanced and strengthened. Going for sub regional cooperation through mutual understanding would be the best way for staying alive and developing the region.

Endnotes

1 Patrick Peebles, *The History of Sri Lanka*, Greenwood Publishing Group, 2006. Also refer Russell R. Ross and Andrea Matles Savada, *Sri Lanka: A Country Study*, Washington: GPO for the Library of Congress, 1988.

2 Stanley Tambiah research concludes that the Sinhalese and the Tamils share many parallel features of "traditional caste, kinship, popular religious cults, customs and so on. But they have come to be divided by their mythic charters and tendentious historical understandings of the past." Refer Stanley J Tambiah, *Sri Lanka: Ethnic Fratricide and the Dismantling of Democracy*, University Of Chicago Press, Chicago, 1991.

3 Devanampiya Tissa became a powerful patron of Buddhism and established the monastery of Maha Vihara, which became the historic center of Theravada Buddhism in Sri Lanka.

4 Jaya Siri Maha Bodhi , available at http://srimahabodhi.org/

5 "Sacred Kapilavastu Relics arriving in Sri Lanka", available at http://www.mea. gov.lk/index.php/en/media/news-archive/3563-sacred-kapilavastu-relics-arriving-in-sri-lanka

6 "When Buddhism was a bridge between Lanka and Tamil Nadu", available at http://www.lakehouse.lk/mihintalava/gaya05.htm

7 Patrick Peebles, *Historical Dictionary of Sri Lanka*, Rowman & Littlefield, October 2015.

8 Keerthi Jayasekera, "Arhant Mahinda in South India and Sri Lanka," *Daily News*, 2 June 2004 at http://archives.dailynews.lk/2004/06/02/fea61.html

9 Lorna Dewaraja, "Cultural relations between Sri Lanka and North India during the Anuradhapura period," *Sri Lanka Journal of Social Sciences*, Vol. 10 (1 &2), 1987, pp. 1-19

10 Refer "Mahavamsa, the great chronicle", *Sunday Observer*, 29 June 2008 at http://www.sundayobserver.lk/2008/06/29/jun03.asp

11 V. Suryanarayan, "Diversities and linkages in Sri Lanka," *The Hindu*, June 06, 2001, http://www.thehindu.com/2001/06/06/stories/05062524.htm

12 Nanda Pethiyagoda Wanasundera, *Cultures of the World – Sri Lanka*, Marshall Cavendish, 2002.

13 A. K. Ananthanathan, *Temple, Religion and Society, East and West*, Vol. 43, No.1/4, 1993, pp. 155-168.

14 Refer for details, S. Pathmanathan, "The Munnesvaram Tamil Inscription of Parākramabāhu VI," *Journal of the Sri Lanka Branch of the Royal Asiatic Society*, New Series, Vol. 18 (1974), pp. 54-69

15 The excavations at Arikamedu, Poompuhar, Korkai and Algankulam in Tamil Nadu have brought to light the evidence of Rouletted Ware which is datable to 2nd-lst century B.C. Arikamedu could be the main centre for the production of the Rouletted pottery in large quantity for trade and domestic uses.

16 Sila Tripati, "Ancient Maritime Trade of the Eastern Indian littoral," *Current Science*, Vol. 100, No. 7, 10 April 2011, pp. 1076-1086.

17 Tyronne Fernando, Alien *Winds across Paradise: A New Look at Sri Lanka's Foreign Relations through the Ages*, Vikas Publishing House, 2002.

18 The Kandyan Convention was signed in Tamil by the King. Tamil was used as one of the court languages. Nayakkar royal family and much of the aristocracy were of South Indian Tamil origin.

19 Lanka Ranaweera, Supannee Kaewsutthi· Aung Win Tun· Hathaichanoke Boonyarit· Samerchai Poolsuwan· and Patcharee Lertrit, "Mitochondrial DNA history of Sri Lankan ethnic people: their relations within the island and with the Indian subcontinental populations," *Journal of Human Genetics*, Vol. 59, 2014, pp. 28–36.

20 Dennis B. McGilvray, "Arabs, Moors and Muslims: Sri Lankan Muslim ethnicity in regional perspective," *Contributions to Indian Sociology*, November 1998, Vol. 32 no. 2, pp. 433-483

21 Heather Devere, "Cross-Cultural Understandings in the Language and Politics of Friendship," *Canadian Social Science*, Vol. 3, No. 6, 2007.

22 Mohamed Mauroof Jameel, *Architectural typological study of coral stone mosques of Maldives*, Masters thesis, University of Malaya, 2012 at http://studentsrepo.um.edu.my/3857/

23 Bethia Nancy Bell and Heather M. Bell, *HCP Bell: archaeologist of Ceylon and the Maldives*, Archetype Publication, 1993.

24 Andrew D.W. Forbes, "Archives and resources for Maldivian history," *South Asia: Journal of South Asian Studies*, Vol. 3, Issue 1, 1980.

25 G.C. Shekhar, "Lanka plays Bengal card - Envoy links Sinhalese to eastern states, TN groups fume," *The Telegraph* (Calcutta), March 29, 2013 at ttp://www.telegraphindia.com/1130329/jsp/nation/story_16723882.jsp

Chapter 4

Maritime Security Tri-lateralism: India, Sri Lanka and Maldives

Dr P K Ghosh

Introduction

India perceives the entire Indian Ocean region (IOR) as its strategic backyard and regards itself as a "security provider" of the region. This view of course is not shared by many, mainly by the Chinese who often state "Indian Ocean is not India's backyard" underlining the fact that they too have deep interests in the region and have been active since they sent their first anti piracy patrol to the Gulf of Aden to fight against Somalian piracy in 2008 as part of the concept of MOOTW (Military Operations other than War)

To reinforce its own perceptions and stem its eroding influence in the region - India has stepped up its efforts in enhancing its relations in general and on maritime security in particular with its island neighbours, an aspect that is being extended to the entire South Asian neighbourhood incrementally. Indeed, it is a process that began some time ago and was essentially pursued by the respective National Security Advisors of the countries which led to the signing of the Trilateral Maritime Security Cooperation Agreement by India, Sri Lanka and the Maldives in July 2013.[1] But undoubtedly the entire effort received an impetus with the March 2015 visit of the Indian Prime Minister Narendra Modi to three island nations, Sri Lanka, Seychelles and Mauritius. A visit to Maldives during the same tour was deliberately avoided in response to the volatile internal politics of the country that had convicted the India backed former President Mohamed Nasheed with a thirteen year prison sentence.

Most analysts and media while dissecting the rationale of the PM's tour tended to project it as a part of a focused effort at veering the host countries away from the growing Chinese influence in the region, but in reality it only represented a part of the larger picture as it carried forward the agenda that had been set in motion earlier by the help of the previous national security advisors (NSA) meetings. With this in background it would be difficult to evaluate if the visit really succeeded in stemming India's eroding influence or did it successfully see a reduction in the evolving Chinese "hold" over the countries.

But the visit did manage to signal India's readiness to assume greater responsibility and overt leadership of the region, in a departure from its earlier ambiguous posture when India was reluctant to assume strategic leadership of the region despite being exhorted by US to do so. Earlier, India had refused to play the role of a regional "headmaster" and preferred to work from the side lines without much fanfare.

India had long harboured great power aspirations as a balancer of power but paradoxically had always refused to take additional responsibility and assume overt leadership in a deeply contested region. Thus, this new post signified a strategic transitioning of sorts. This process of change commenced with India initiating the Indian Ocean Naval Symposium (IONS) maritime initiative wherein it played the role of an "unobtrusive fulcrum".[2] Hence, the overt manifestations were much more in evidence in the current case of "maritime security trilateralism" highlighted during the Modi visit.

At the heart of this is new posturing is the Indian desire to build a multi-lateral maritime arrangement with Sri Lanka, Seychelles, Mauritius and Maldives. "We call this Indian Ocean outreach as 'SAGAR' said Prime Minister Modi in Mauritius during his visit. At another occasion the Foreign Minister added "We seek a future for Indian Ocean that lives up to the name of SAGAR- Security and Growth for All in the Region." [3] However, it is noteworthy that - India, Sri Lanka and Maldives have not been comfortable with the concept of a security alliance either in substance or in terms and hence have avoided the same amongst themselves or with others. Interestingly none joined the earlier security constructs like the Southeast Asia Treaty Organisation (SEATO) or Central Treaty Organisation (CENTO). Hence, the coming together of these nations on a security related platform signifies the evolving geo politics of the region and the national priorities of the countries involved.

The NSA level Meetings earlier hadn't involved all the islands together and the main agenda was simply to create a closer functional operative only on maritime security within the given three islands (to be later expanded to other islands as well). Given that all the islands in the region lacked maritime capacity, India stepped in to promise in assisting in capacity build-up. Thus, the focus essentially was to bring these countries within a common grid of a multilateral maritime security framework, reiterating India's new policy of 'neighbours first.'

Factors contributing to Maritime Security Trilateral

There were many factors which contributed to the formation of the trilateral network. The primary one which provided the impetus was the maritime challenges faced by the countries were similar if not identical. Asymmetric threats such as maritime terrorism, arms and drug trade, piracy, human and arms smuggling, were essentially transnational in characteristics requiring multinational response strategies – which made it incumbent on India with its large maritime capacity to provide the lead as well as help in building maritime capacity of its friendly neighbours.

Apart from such threats the necessity of maintaining an advanced level of Maritime Domain awareness (MDA) as part of the overall response strategy was another aspect which led to the focus on the sharing of technical aspects of MDA. IOR being the hub of many natural calamities – the brunt of which had often been faced by the littorals, it was inevitable that disaster management and Humanitarian Assistance and Disaster Relief (HADR) become a factor that brought the countries together. With Indian forces providing yeoman services during the Tsunami of 2004 – it was natural for India to assume leadership in this regard.

Apart from the above, the dire need to ensure Sea Lanes of Communication (SLOC) security and unhindered passage of maritime trade was another aspect that helped in coming together of the countries, since all the littorals were deeply dependent on maritime trade for their own economic well being . Similarly, the increasing role of China in fostering its bilateral relations with the island neighbours was one of the most important factors strategically to initiate this movement. The Indians perceive such moves by China in their strategic backyard as being inimical to their interests. The numerous construction projects of ports, infrastructure and base facilities in the IOR by China is a matter of great concern for India as it diminishes its strategic leverages. The construction of Hambantota port in Sri Lanka with Chinese money and material and anchoring of Ming class diesel submarine at a private dock in Colombo port, built, controlled and run by a Chinese company, the China Merchants Holdings (international) with the Sri Lankan administered harbor, is a case in point[4]. It is probably for this reason that New Delhi is apprehensive about China's "Maritime Silk Route" concept.

India's Security Relations with Sri Lanka

The India Prime Minter's visit to Sri Lanka held deep significance as it was the first one in 28 years and it occurred at a time when China's growing presence in Sri Lanka had suffered a setback with the defeat of Mahinda Rajapaksa. Earlier, considerable amount of heartburn had resulted from Rajapaksha's perceptible tilt towards China. A series of incidents had convinced the Indian Government that it needed serious discussion with the Sri Lankans on the issue as the repeated docking of Chinese submarines at harbour had caused serious security concerns for India. Fortunately for India, a subsequent change in government brought respite and the new Sirisena government has made its desire publicly to correct the earlier tilt towards China and has already made some significant overtures towards India. The new President has visited India as his first trip abroad which resulted in a civil nuclear energy cooperation pact between India and Sri Lanka. In a move that risks diplomatic row with is largest trading partner, Sri Lanka has suspended a $1.4 billion Chinese luxury real estate project in Colombo.[5]

Having overcome the baggage of history, it needs to be mentioned that the two armed forces of India and Sri Lanka support a close service to service relationship. Training exchanges at differing levels of seniority have been common and continue to be popularly subscribed. Military intelligence sharing has continued since earlier times when on several occasions such information helped the Sri Lankan Navy to successfully intercept arms shipments to the LTTE.

However, paradoxically despite the close Defence cooperation between the countries, one of the biggest unfinished agendas has been the absence of a formal Defence Cooperation Agreement (DCA) even though it has been in discussion since 2003. Domestic compulsions on either side have prevented the final signing of the DCA.[6] The encouraging aspect, however, has been that the lack of a formal defence agreement has not been a real constraining factor in enhancing the level of defence cooperation between the two countries. For example despite a political controversy that erupted in Tamil Nadu in 2013, India continues to train Sri Lankan personnel and officers.[7] Additionally, New Delhi and Colombo have also commenced a formal Annual Defence Dialogue (ADD) in February 2012.

In the field of equipment transfers, even though India has steadfastly maintained its public posturing about not supplying offensive military hardware to Sri Lanka, it has quietly decided to extend a 100 million dollars credit line for purchase of non-lethal weapons.[8] In fact since 2000, India has supplied 24 L-70 anti-aircraft guns, 11 USFM radars, 10 Mine Protected Vehicles and 24 Battlefield Surveillance Radars to Sri Lanka.

India's Security Relations with Maldives

India and Maldives both have developed close strategic, military, economic and cultural relations over the many years. The closeness was particularly evident when India intervened militarily at the request of the President of Maldives and prevented a coup in November 1988. Operation Cactus as it was termed was a success and prevented the overthrow of President Gayoom by a Maldivian named Abdullah Luthufi and his group assisted by 80 heavily armed mercenaries of the People's Liberation Organisation of Tamil Eelam (PLOTE). On request from President Gayoom the Indian government dispatched 1600 troops by air who finally overcame the mercenaries and prevented the coup. The event firmly established India's role as a security provider in the entire region as New Delhi's role was well appreciated by the international community.

The reiteration that India was emerging as a security provider came up again when Maldives approached New Delhi in 2009, over fears that one of its island resorts could be taken over by terrorists given its lack of military and surveillance capabilities.[9] In the meantime, due to an agreement signed in 2009 the following actions had already been initiated

a) India has permanently based two helicopters at Maldives for surveillance. One advanced Advanced Light Helicopter (ALH) based in Addu Island and the other more advanced helicopter to be based in Hannimadhoo Island.

b) Maldives has coastal radars on only two of its 26 atolls. India helped in setting up radars stations in all 26 for seamless coverage

c) The coastal radar chain in Maldives will be networked with the Indian coastal radar system. India has already undertaken a project to install radars along its entire coastline. The radar chains are being interlinked and a central control room in India's Coastal Command.

In addition to the above defence arrangements the Indian Coast Guard (ICG) has been tasked to utilise its Dornier aircraft for regular surveillance sorties over the island. The aim is to have active air surveillance and patrolling against the emergent threat from Somali pirates and these Dornier sorties have helped in easing the threat perception. Besides, India-Maldives-Sri Lanka also held a Joint trilateral Coast Guard exercise called DOSTI XI off the coast of Male (Maldives) in April 2012[10] which looked at areas of common interest and enhanced interoperability between the forces.

Earlier NSA Meetings and its Outcome

The process of trilateralism had actually commenced with the intensive staff level talks that were followed by the NSA level talks which provided the impetus for the initiative and in the development of a trilateral security partnership and the Agreement. The first such meeting was held in Male in October 2011 which had preceded four separate meetings of senior officials between the three sides. This preparatory work by the working level was useful in framing the outcomes of the Second NSA-level Trilateral Meeting.[11]

The second meeting of the NSA was hosted by Sri Lanka and held in Colombo in July 2013. The three participating countries agreed on a roadmap for cooperation in maritime security, comprising the following three categories of activities:

- Initiatives to enhance Maritime Domain Awareness (MDA) especially initiatives such as Long Range Identification and Tracking (LRIT) services and sharing of Automatic Identification System (AIS) data;

- Training and capacity building initiatives in areas of MDA, Search and Rescue, and Oil Pollution Response; and

- Joint activities including trilateral exercises, maintaining lines of communication on illegal maritime activities, formulation of marine oil pollution response contingency plans and cooperation in legal and policy issues related to piracy.[12]

India hosted the third NSA-level Trilateral Meeting on Maritime Security Cooperation between Maldives, Sri Lanka and India on 6 March 2014 in New Delhi. The same three primary interlocutors who had participated in the earlier meetings did so this time. Accordingly Indian team was led by Ambassador Shivshankar Menon, while the Maldivian side was headed by Col(Retd) Mohamed Nazim, Minister of Defence (MoD) and National Security and Mr Gotabaya Rajapaksa, Secretary, MoD and Urban Development of Sri Lanka headed the his country's delegation . The important aspect was that the meeting was also attended by Mauritius and Seychelles which implied that they too would become part of the grouping.

This meeting basically discussed the progress of implementation of various activities that had been identified earlier. They also discussed new areas of cooperation including hydrography; training in Visit, Board, Search and Seizure Operations; training on board Indian Sail Training Ships; exchanges between think tanks; and joint participation in adventure activities.[13] Given India's horrific experience with the Mumbai blasts- there was a realization that – terrorism was a trans national crime that demanded the active participation of all littorals whose maritime capacity needed to built as there a dire necessity to invest in MDA – specifically Long Range Identification and Tracking (LRIT) and the Automatic Identification System (AIS). Thus, it provided India with the unique opportunity to share its technological expertise with its allies for maritime capacity enhancement.

The other topics of discussion included Search and Rescue (SAR). It was agreed that India would also provide expertise and technical assistance for setting up/ enhancing Maritime Rescue Coordination Centres (MRCCs) in Sri Lanka[14] and Maldives for effective coordination in relaying and receiving distress alerts and safety messages. Given the current focus on preventing / controlling maritime pollution that not only to destroys marine environment but has considerable security considerations- this was another topic for discussion. With Indian Coast Guard (INCG) and US Coast Guard being the few maritime agencies that were capable of tackling oil pollution it was decided that there was considerable scope for promoting marine oil pollution response cooperation with the appropriate agencies of these island nations.

One of the most important issues that was discussed was the rise of asymmetric challenges especially terrorism and piracy in the region. Both these aspects scored high in the threat perception of the participating littorals. As a consequence there were extensive discussions on the need to expand 'DOSTI' (friendship) exercises[15] by holding table top exercises and further enhancing sharing of the information on illegal maritime activities through existing points of contact. Additionally, there was also a consensus on forming a trilateral sub-group which would focus exclusively on the complexities of policy and legal issues related to piracy. With India having been unable to finally pass a national legislation (Piracy Bill 2012) to overcome a serious hurdle in prosecution of apprehended pirates - this was an issue that was significant in dealing with anti- piracy operations.

These meetings chalked out the entire roadmap for future security cooperation outlining the following:

a. The facility of the Indian Long Range Identification and Tracking (LRIT) Data Centre to be used by Sri Lanka and Maldives in order to monitor and track their merchant vessels flying their flags. In turn Sri Lanka and Maldives are to provide required details of their merchant ships as per International Maritime Organisation (IMO) regulations.

b. The Merchant Ship Information System (MSIS) be utilized for exchange of unclassified information on shipping;

c. Sharing Automatic Identification System (AIS) data in a trilateral format over the MSIS platform;

d. Undertaking MDA training in India;

e. Strengthening maritime linkages in the field of SAR through operations, providing expertise and technical assistance by India in setting up Maritime Rescue Coordination Centres (MRCCs) in Sri Lanka and Maldives, coordination in relaying and receiving distress alerts and safety messages, and, conduct of SAR training in India;

f. Strengthening mechanisms for Exclusive Economic Zone (EEZ) surveillance and providing additional support and assets on a case by case basis;

g. Maintaining lines of communication on illegal maritime activities between identified Points of Contact and exchanging messages on a regular basis;

h. Strengthening marine pollution response cooperation through conduct of IMO Level I and Level II courses in India, formulating contingency plans for pollution response, capacity building, and participating in India's National Pollution Response Exercise (NATPOLREX), as observers;

i. Strengthening the biennial trilateral exercise 'DOSTI' by conducting table top exercises and seminars on maritime issues in every alternate year;

j. Passing Tsunami warnings simultaneously to agreed Points of Contact and also to the designated National Tsunami Warning Centres;

k. Setting up a trilateral sub-group focused on legal and policy issues related to piracy.

Beyond Trilateralism

The concept of comprehensive security in modern usage has an accent on cooperative approaches but using and sharing of latest technology in capacity building is a relatively new idea within the IOR especially for India which was hindered by its previous isolationistic mindset that was prominent during the Cold war era. Undoubtedly, the success of getting its island neighbours within maritime security grid will be expanded further in due course of time – as is evident from the willingness of the other islands to follow suit. Given that these islands face similar maritime challenges such a symbiotic arrangement seems mutually beneficial to all. Thus very soon Mauritius and Seychelles, which share strong bilateral relations with India, are most likely to join in this arrangement.

Strategically, the Indians have been wary of the growing influence of the external powers in the region – mainly with respect to China. Hence at the subterranean level, this dynamic arrangement will partly offset the growing influence of China and Pakistan in the regional dynamics. Additionally, the current arrangement will provide India with the option to develop forward bases in the entire region if the need arises. With the available technology and the willingness of the participating countries these bases could well be notional or real. Thus, in a master stroke it will enable India to retain it public posturing against military forward basing in the region and thus maintain moral high ground – while possessing the ability to assess the farthest regions with technological means without the overwhelming physical presence of its military troops in that area.

The task is likely to be made easier since India is normally perceived as a benign power in the Indian Ocean, in sharp contrast to the perception of a hegemonic China which supports an intrusive way of providing aid and capacity building assistance. Hence, it might be easier for the littorals to readily join the bandwagon willingly rather than be swayed by Chinese inducements. Admittedly, there exists another major maritime security initiative known as the Indian Ocean Naval Symposium (IONS), initiated by India in 2008 that aims at bringing the IOR littoral navies together for active discussions on matters of common maritime interest. [16] However, this regional forum of navies is decidedly naval in its outlook and can supplement a more holistic overview of security cooperation in the region. With a perceptible "cooling" of IONS ability to gather other littorals in enhancing the maritime dialogue- such trilateral or multi lateral agreements are more potent and effective in achieving their objective. [17]

Conclusion

The importance of the Mahanian concept of utilising Sea Power for achievement of national objectives has led to the realization amongst a normally 'sea blind' Indian bureaucracy to become more pro active. It is now being understood that naval diplomacy and projection of maritime power can help India in achieve its objectives of being a net security provider in a region perceived to be its strategic backyard. With this background the rise of maritime threats from the seas and the lack of maritime capacity amongst many friendly littorals has resulted in a symbiotic relationship of sorts and resulted in India drawing close two of its neighbouring islands. The first step in this regard has been the signing of the security related Trilateral Maritime Security Cooperation Agreement by India, Sri Lanka and the Maldives with such an arrangement to be expanded to all its friendly island neighbours.

Simultaneously, these efforts have helped India to stem its own eroding influence in the region while denuding the increasing influence of foreign powers, mainly China in the region. Strategically India's initiative 'neighbours first' policy that has regionally manifested into getting the friendly island nations on a common maritime security grid has strenuously reiterated India's position as a net security provider. This has also ensured that India retains strategic leverages against adversarial powers that have been active in fostering their influence in the region. However, it remains to be seen how far India can nourish this symbiotic relations with its neighbours and continue offsetting the Chinese influence in the years to come.

Endnotes

1   "Sri Lanka signs maritime cooperation Agreement with India and Maldives" available at http://www.srilankaembassy.be/old/HomePagePhoto/2013/Doc36.pdf

2   P K Ghosh, "Indian Ocean dynamics: An Indian perspective", *East Asia Forum*, 5 April 2011, available at: http://www.eastasiaforum.org/2011/04/05/indian-ocean-dynamics-an-indian-perspective/

3   As stated by Foreign Minster External Affairs Minister Sushma Swaraj at the inauguration of an International Conference on "India and Indian Ocean: Renewing the Maritime Trade and Civilisational linkages" 20 March 2015, available at: http://pib.nic.in/newsite/PrintRelease.aspx?relid=117542

4   Abjijit Singh, 'China's "Maritime Bases" in the IOR: A Chronicle of Dominance Foretold', *Strategic Analysis*, Strategic Analysis, Vol. 39, No. 3, 2015, pp. 293-297.

5   The Sri Lankan government's decision to review, and in effect suspend, the $US1.4 billion, Chinese-backed Colombo Port City (CPC) project strained relations between Beijing and Colombo considerably. The plan was to construct a modern 500-acre (230 hectare) city, with hotels, apartments and office buildings, on earth fill near the seafront of Colombo harbor. About 200 acres were to be held by China Communications Construction Company (CCCC), the main contractor, on a 99-year lease. The deal was sealed during Rajpaksha's time. Also see Manusha Fernando "Sri Lanka-China tensions rise over suspended port project" 16 March 2015, available at https://www.wsws. org/en/articles/2015/03/16/chin-m16.html

6   Nitin Gokhale "Army Chief Visits Colombo to Further Indo Sri Lanka ties" 19 Dec 2012, available at http://www.ndtv.com/article/india/army-chief-visits-colombo-to-further-indo-sri-lankan-defence-ties-307133

7   "India Sri Lanka Defence Cooperation", available at <http://ecurrentaffairs.in/ blog/india-srilanka-defence-cooperation/>

8   Ibid

9   Manu Pubby, " India Bringing Maldives into its Security net "Indian Express August 13, 2009, available at http://www.indianexpress.com/news/India-bringing-Maldives-into-its-security-net/501583

10 "Joint Statement by India and Maldives on the Visit of the President of Maldives to India" May 14, 2012, available at http://mea.gov.in/bilateral-documents. htm?dtl/19869/Joint+Statement+by+India+and+Maldives+on+the+Visit+of+ the+President+of+Maldives+to+India

11 "Outcome Document of the Second NSA-Level Meeting on Trilateral Cooperation on Maritime Security between India, the Maldives and Sri Lanka," July 09, 2013, available at http://www.mea.gov.in/bilateral-documents. htm?dtl/21922/Outcome+Document+of+the+Second+NSALevel+Meeting+o n+Trilateral+Cooperation+on+Maritime+Security+between+India+the+Mal dives+and+Sri+Lanka

12 "NSA level meeting on trilateral Maritime Security Cooperation between India, Sri Lanka and Maldives" 06th March 2014, available at MEA website http://mea.gov.in/in-focus-article.htm?23037/NSA+level+meeting+on+trilate ral+Maritime+Security+Cooperation+between+India+Sri+Lanka+and+Mald ives

13 Ibid

14 India currently has three MRCCs (at Mumbai, Chennai and at Port Blair) in its Search and Rescue Region (SRR) as well as numerous Maritime Rescue Sub Centres (MRSC's) There exists an MRCC in Colombo

15 Exercise "Dosti" (Friendship) was started as a bi-annual exercise between the Coast Guards of India and Maldives in 1991 with the objective of strengthening co-operation. In its 20th year it included (2012) the Sri Lankan Coast Guard.

16 For a detailed treatment see P K Ghosh " Indian Ocean Naval Symposium: Uniting the Maritime Indian Ocean Region", *Strategic Analysis* 36(3) May June 2012 pp. 352-357

17 See P K Ghosh "IONS and the Indian Ocean : Reviving a Listless Initiative", *RSIS Commentary* No.083/2014 dated 08 May 2014

Chapter 5

Trade and Development in India's Engagements with Sri Lanka and Maldives: Emerging Trends

Shaji S

India's engagement in the Indian Ocean has undergone many changes in recent times with increased involvement of economic, strategic and cultural ties with countries in the region which include littoral and continental states. This was manifested against the backdrop of increasing emphasis on sub-regionalism which assumed paramount significance as reflected in debates and discussions in the Eighteenth SAARC Summit at Kathmandu, Nepal in November 2014. In fact, sub-regionalism has emerged as a new solution to tide over problems that emanated from the roadblocks on the onward march of macro-level regionalism (the whole region wise) in South Asia. In view of this, the work analyses the increasing role that trade and development plays in India's relationship with island states such as Sri Lanka and Maldives. First section of the chapter analyses the changing setting of regionalism/sub-regionalism in South Asia in the backdrop of emerging power dynamics in the region. The second section of the chapter analyses India's engagement with Sri Lanka and Maldives by way of the trade and developmental initiatives. The third section discusses trilateralism[1] in which India is involved with Sri Lanka and Maldives and its emerging possibilities.

Regionalism in South Asia has been largely shaped by the developments at the global (systemic) and domestic (unit) level factors. The global level factors consist of expansion of the processes of globalisation and domestic level factors primarily connected to economic and strategic interests. The processes of globalisation triggered a series of integration processes at different geographic locations around the world which directly and indirectly influenced South Asian region too. Against this setting, the next section discusses regionalism and its intricate relations with processes of globalisation, its influence in South Asian initiatives on regionalism while analysing its implications for India's foreign policy.

Regionalism and Sub-regionalism in South Asia: A General Setting

The dismantling of binaries associated with the Cold War in the early 1990s and the onset of capitalism on the global stage as the dominant model of economic development reshaped policies of states, especially in the developing world. Asian States such as India and China were no exception to such a trend. The expansion of market oriented models forced them to give importance to accessing natural resources such as oil and minerals as well as reaching out to the markets of new destinations which became priority in policy discourses.[2] In fact, such changes in priorities had implications for the relations of Asian States like India and China had with the rest of the world. In this context, since the end of Cold War, India has re-oriented its foreign policy premises such as non-alignment by shedding political emphasis to give thrust to economic aspects. Parallel to that, India has forged new alliances, re-energised traditional relations and provided new dynamism to regional groupings while breaking new pathways.[3] Out of these, there has been a special emphasis on regionalism.

In such a scheme of things, as stated before, regionalism has assumed paramount significance in the foreign policy of India. In a way, since 1990s, India has been emphasising on 'regionalism', a manifestation of how India can respond to changes in the global architecture of politics and economy after the end of Cold War, by changing its policies and strategies at the external front while making substantial economic and governance reforms at the domestic front. There were several attempts to operationalize such a strategy (emphasis on regionalism) as evident from India's attempt to form several regional blocs such as Bay of Bengal Initiative for Multi-sectoral Technical and Economic Cooperation (BIMSTEC), Indian Ocean Rim–Association for Regional Cooperation (IOR-ARC),South Asian Free Trade Agreement (SAFTA) as well as formulating regional policies such as 'Look East Policy',[4]while restructuring its economy at the domestic front through privatisation, liberalisation and globalisation. Before getting into the nuances of sub-regionalism, let us examine the background of regionalism and economic cooperation in South Asia where India and other regional states are involved in.

Background to Regionalism and Economic Cooperation in South Asia

Since 1990s, regionalism in South Asia involving India and other states is largely influenced by developments at the global level which began to unfold since late 1980s (the processes of globalisation).At the global level, there was substantial hike in the flow of capital to the emerging market economies, which in turn unfolded both problems and promises. One of the implications of this development was the intensification of interdependence among states and heightening of the perception of that interdependence. Such processes resulted in regional economic integration efforts like the European Union (EU), the North America Free Trade Agreement (NAFTA) and the Asia Pacific Economic Cooperation (APEC), to name a few examples of this heightened perception of interdependence. In the South Asian region, regional integration has taken solid shape through South Asian Association for Regional Co-operation (SAARC).

In a way, India's involvement in the regionalisation process got a boost in the post-Cold War phase. In many ways, regionalism, besides its strategic, geo-political and foreign policy dimensions, has been a major plank of development co-operation and integration in many parts of the world. There are several examples of varieties of regional groupings that have transformed the conventional outlook and aspirations into more open, dynamic and wider systems and practices of peaceful co-existence, collective responsibility and regional development.

Emphasis on regionalism provided several benefits to states like India. It offered itself as a strategy to compete with other states with regard to the acquisition of technology, resources and accessing market in the era of globalisation. India has invariably followed the same trajectory. Indeed, regionalisation has become one of the instruments employed by states like India to cope with the realities of globalisation. Globalisation and the rapid emergence of market economies all over the world from Southeast Asia to Latin America have resulted in the spectacular emergence of regional co-operation and integration.[5]Due to several complex and contentious political, economic, ethnic and territorial issues, India had overlooked the needs and possibilities of building strong regional groupings in the past (till the beginning of 1990s).

However, the end of Cold War, coupled with the processes of globalisation, has prompted India to effectively formulate and participate in regional groupings. Apart from serving the economic interests in the region, these groupings can act as an effective medium to control the adverse effects of free markets created by World Trade Organisation (WTO). For instance, within the region, the technology and capital can be traded among the member states of a regional grouping, which reduces the cost of purchasing technology from transnational corporations and developed states. This notion has resulted in building of several institutional mechanisms within the framework of South Asian Association of Regional Cooperation (SAARC).In South Asia, as a prelude to South Asian Free Trade Area; the SAARC Preferential Trading Arrangement (SAAPTA) came into existence in December 1995. Consequently, intra-regional trade improved drastically. The intra-SAARC trade recorded an average annual growth rate of 31.06 per cent during the period 1990-2001 as against a very low growth rate of 3.4 per cent during the period 1980-1990. On the other end, South Asia's trade with states outside the region grew at the rate of 11.83 and 8.15 per cent respectively during the same period. As a result, intra-SAARC trade, as percentage of South Asia's world trade has recorded an upward trend from 2.42 per cent in 1990 to 4.56 per cent in 2001. At present, the intra-regional trade is around 5 per cent (2014-2015).[6] The SAARC Summit, which was held in July 1998, addressed issues pertaining to low intra-regional trade at length and decided to institute a free trade area in the region (South Asia Free Trade Area). The 12th SAARC Summit held in Islamabad in January 2004 signed a framework agreement on South Asian Free Trade Area (SAFTA), which was proposed to be implemented from 2006 onwards. Indeed, it came into existence in 2006, but it is not fully operational yet. It is expected to be operational from 2016 by lowering tariffs in a phased manner.

The broader objectives of the proposed free trade was directed at promoting free trade and competitiveness among member states and it was assumed that the Free Trade Area would induce foreign states and groups to establish their industries in the region that can bring home sufficient foreign direct investment (FDI), the major source of technology. According to J.N Dixit, creating a South Asian Common Market, constructing transnational transportation system by road, rail, air and ships along the coastal sea lines together with purposive planning to further cooperation in the sphere of developing and distributing energy resources are the longer-term objectives which states of SAARC should take cognizance of and cooperate in a creative manner to meet these tasks.[7] There were several attempts on the part of leaderships in South Asia to materialize such objectives. Here, the Gujral Doctrine of 1998 deserves special mention. The Gujral Doctrine consisted of the pursuance of a policy of non-reciprocity towards neighbouring states with the idea of accommodating their interests (excluding Pakistan). It was based on the fact that being the most powerful state in South-Asia, India needs to play a conciliatory and accommodative role vis-à-vis its neighbours in the larger interests of maintaining peace and stability in the region.[8] To impart momentum to this trade grouping, India offered concessions on 500 consumer goods from least developed states in the region.

Another interesting development regarding regionalism in South Asia was SAARC forming a Committee -Group of Eminent Persons (GEP) to develop a long-range vision and formulate a perspective plan of action including the agenda for the millennium and spell out the targets to be achieved by the year 2020. The GEP provided a very comprehensive and a clear road map. It envisaged the implementation of SAFTA in the year 2008 (which did not materialize). It also envisaged a SAARC Customs Union by 2015 and a SAARC Economic Union by 2020. In fact, the establishment of an Economic Union was considered to be an ideal situation in South Asian States where technology and FDI can be easily traded without any hassles. In short, the end of the Cold War and the subsequent emergence of economic ideology of North as the moving force in international relations, and the setting up of WTO provided an altogether new dynamism for regional cooperation in South Asia.

In addition to regional trade and economic initiatives, the global trade and economic issues are also prioritised by SAARC countries. For instance, the WTO related issues were also taken seriously by the SAARC member states as a collective voice and effort. A joint statement was released by the SAARC commerce ministers in Male in August 1999. This was issued with a view to adopting a common position in advance of the Third WTO

Ministerial Meeting at Seattle in 1999. In a way, India's strategy, at present, is to fight the hegemonic tendencies of developed states as well as appropriate the opportunities thrown by WTO.

Another prominent regional grouping in which India joined after 1990s by involving several South Asian and Indian Ocean states was the Indian Ocean Rim Association for Regional Co-operation (IOR-ARC) in 1997. This policy was envisaged to enhance co-operation in bilateral and in multilateral levels, especially in economic matters. If implemented in the proper direction, this can make big strides in technological and economic co-operation among South-Asian states. The second initiative of India in the South and South East Asia was Bengal Initiative for Multi-sectoral Technical and Economic Cooperation (BIMSTEC) by involving states such as Thailand, Bangladesh, Sri Lanka and so on. The BIMSTEC process marked a new phase in India's Look East policy (a policy aimed at regionalism). In short, the Government, led by P.V Narasimha Rao launched this initiative towards South East Asia in the early 1990s. Atal Behari Vajpayee as Prime Minister (1999-2004) deepened the scope and substance of India's Look East policy to cover much of Asia, including the ASEAN, China, Japan, Australia and New Zealand. The first phase of the Look East Policy focused on developing commercial relations and institutional links with Asia. In the second phase of the Look East policy, India is aiming at political partnerships, physical connectivity through road and rail links, free trade arrangements, and defence co-operation.[9] There are certain positive impacts that emanated out of these initiatives (India's increased linkages with South East Asian states), especially achieving connectivity between India and South East Asian States by road, air and sea in the recent times. Having examined these macro level regional initiatives, the next section discusses certain challenges that regional integration initiatives such as SAARC face and subsequent notions unfolded under sub regional frame works such as India- Sri Lanka-Maldives Trilateralism.

India's Interest in Trilaterlaism involving Sri Lanka and Maldives

SAARC and other macro level regional initiatives though created a positive impression in the first few decades since its origin, was influenced by an array of political conflicts that emanated out of bilateral issues involving South Asian states, primarily between India and Pakistan. Such impediments/challenges slowed down the macro level processes and therefore fewer benefits emerged out of it as evident from low rate of intra-regional trade, less connectivity and mobility across national boundaries. Subsequently, sub-regional initiatives have emerged as a manifestation of impediments on the path of furthering regionalism. In a way 'sub-regionalism' has several potentials (from India's standpoint): it can provide boost to India's trade and development which in a way can transform South Asia into a major hub of trade in the South Asian region. In addition, India is likely to benefit out of increased market access, trade, investment and increased mobility for the people across national boundaries.[10]

In such a scenario, India began to develop sub-regional initiatives in the region. The history of sub-regionalism can be traced to Council of Ministers' Meeting of SAARC where the notion of 'sub regionalism' was endorsed, for the first time, in 1996[11] (which got an official endorsement in Male Summit of 1997).This idea got further acceptance when India, Nepal, Bangladesh and Bhutan together proposed sub regional cooperation on six areas, prominently on multi-model transport and energy. In fact, from 2007 onwards, more emphasis was given on multi-mode transportation, to operationalize sub-regionalism. The endorsing and signing of the much awaited Motor Vehicles Agreement (BBIN MVA) by the Transport Ministers of the BBIN (Bangladesh, Bhutan, India and Nepal) countries on 15 June at Thimphu is being considered as a 'benchmark' for sub-regionalism in South Asia.[12]Similarly, India, Sri Lanka, Maldives Maritime Trilateralism is another initiative in this regard.

Such an initiative is partially influenced by several factors, out of which increasing foot print of China in the region is a major one. In a way, during last few years, Sri Lankan and Maldives Government have been showing affinity towards China in a big way, especially in the realm of trade and security related matters. The then President Mahindra Rajapaksa and the Maldivian Leadership have tried to move closer to China by way of their policies and strategies. For instance, Maldives's new Land Act was seen an attempt to favor Chinese interest. China is likely to benefit from the new Land acquisition act in Maldives which has provision of investing US $1billion with 70 per cent land claiming.[13] It is perceived that such provisions are deliberately created to benefit Chinese interest, as some scholars observe. At the same time, Maldivian leadership is assuring India that Maldivian land will not be used against the interests of India. However, there is a perception that Chinese foray into Maldives in the contemporary times is part of China's long term plan of building a Maritime Silk Route (MSR). Of late, Chinese trade and investment are steadily increasing with Maldives. In the realm of trade, bilateral trade between China and Maldives stood at $ 64 million in 2010 and increased to $98 million in 2013.[14] China is also investing in major infrastructure sectors such as roads, telecommunication, housing as well as renewal energy, tourism and so on. Out of these, one of the major Chinese investments in Maldives is a Bridge Project connecting the island in which new airport is situated with the capital of Maldives. In addition, Chinese tourists are the largest tourist contingent in Maldives whose number has increased from 12,000 in 2010 to 333,000 in 2013.[15]Around 30 to 40 per cent of tourists to Maldives are from China. In addition, Maldives entered into an Agreement with China's Asian Infrastructure Investment Bank.[16] This was basically undertaken to support the proposed infrastructural projects of Maldives. In this context, the next section examines India's role in furthering bilateral ties especially in the realm of trade involving Sri Lanka and Maldives.

Indian Engagements with Sri Lanka and Maldives through Trade and development

India's engagement in Indian Ocean has undergone changes in recent times with increased involvement of economic, strategic and cultural ties with neighbouring island states. This is reflected in an increased frequency of visits by political leaderships of the both countries as well as quantum of trade and business. India's ties with Sri Lanka and Maldives have increased substantially in the recent times in the region which includes littoral and continental states. As far as Sri Lanka is concerned, India is its leading trading partner with bilateral trade standing at $4.6 billion in 2014.[17]The last decade has witnessed drastic increase in Indo-Sri Lankan trade as evident from the jump from $655 million to $ 3636 million in 2013.

More recently, in the realm of trade, there has been a huge hike in export and import between India and Sri Lanka. For instance, India's export to Sri Lanka has gone up from Rs. 1,595,089.35 Lakhs in 2010-11 to Rs. 4,103,801.13 in the year 2014-15 period registering a 48 per cent increase between the period mentioned. In the same period, India's import from Sri Lanka too increased from Rs.227, 873.44 lakhs to Rs. 464,275.90 lakhs, a growth of 14 per cent (Annexure 1).

In addition, in the case of Sri Lanka, the last few years have also witnessed an increasing trend of Sri Lankan Investments in India. The notable example consist of Ceylon Biscuits (Munchee Brand), Carlsberg, Brandix (the company plans an investment of $1 Billion in Vishakhapatnam in the future), MAS Holding, John Keels, Heylees. The Indo-Sri Lankan trade has gone up in the recent times as the political climate in the island state changed drastically after the end of civil war. Indo-Sri Lankan trade is currently at US$4 Billion. Major Sri Lankan products imported to India include Spices, Natural Rubber, Electrical and Electronic Equipment, Paper, Ships and Boats whereas Indian products exported to Sri Lanka include Motor Vehicles, Minerals and Iron, Pharmaceuticals, Cotton, Chemicals, Cement, Finished fabrics and so on.[18]Most of Sri Lanka's export to India is carried within the framework of India-Sri Lanka Free Trade Agreement (ISFTA) whereas India's export to Sri Lanka is mostly carried out outside the framework of ISFTA.[19]India has been insisting on the signing of Comprehensive Economic Partnership Agreement (CEPA) which in a way is presumed to be a transformation from ISFTA which India signed with Sri Lanka in 2000.

Similarly, in the case of Maldives, to increase its strategic presence and cooperation in the Indian Ocean Region, India signed a bilateral pact with the Maldives in August 2009, which envisaged the setting up of a network of 26 radars across the Maldives' 26 atolls. Such an arrangement will be linked to the Indian coastal command to effectively monitor the vast uninhabited Maldivian islands against possible terrorist intrusion and activities of piracy in its EEZ. India has also contributed to the capacity-building efforts in the island state. This was accompanied by the increasing volume of trade which began in a structured way after India signed a trade agreement with Maldives in 1981.

In the developmental front, State Bank of India has been contributing to the development of the Island State by way of offering loans to different entrepreneurs. Major Indian companies like Tata are involved in the construction of Low Cost Housing Project.[20] The other companies such as Tatwa Global renewal Energy, Daewoo, Innovative Parking Solutions and so on are also involved in various sectors such as waste management, construction of multi-storey buildings and so on.[21] All these developments have also contributed to the increased trade.

As stated earlier, the trade between India and Maldives has also grown substantially over a period of time. For instance, the combined trade between both the countries was Rs.377.22 crores in 2007 which increased up to more than Rs. 700 crores by 2013.[22] India had also come to the rescue of Maldives when its one and only Sewage Plant was damaged due to fire which rendered around one lakh people left without drinking water.[23] In addition, India helped setting up of various institutions such as– Indira Gandhi Memorial Hospital (IGMH), Maldives Institute of Technical Education (MITE) and so on.[24] However, GMR episode in which Maldivian Government cancelled the contract to GMR led consortium to construct Maldives Airport in 2012, had brought the relationship between two countries to a fragile point.[25]

However, in the case of India's trade with Maldives, India's trade has grown up from Rs.45,554.05 in the year 2010-2011 to Rs. 93,314.67 in 2014-2015 registering an increase of 45.13 per cent. In the same period, India's import has declined from Rs.14,543.27 to Rs. 2,648.42 which is actually a drop of 82 per cent (Annexure 2).[26] In the trade spectrum involving India and Maldives, India imports scrap metals from Maldives while its exports include agriculture and poultry produce, sugar, fruits, vegetables, spices, rice, flour (atta), textiles, drugs and medicines, a variety of engineering and industrial products, sand and aggregate cement for construction, etc.[27]

In the recently concluded agreement (2011) between India and Maldives, both countries agreed to focus on building health infrastructure in Maldives. In addition, they plan to work towards rigorous economic cooperation in several sectors such as food security, tourism, fisheries development, transportation, information technology, new and renewal energy, communication, banking and financial sectors. They have also decided to improve credit and insurance facilities and assistance in the establishment of development of financial institutions. India has promised financial support to Maldives for several cooperation and developmental projects, including the setting up of Maldives Police Academy, the renovation of the Indira Gandhi Memorial Hospital (IGMH) established by Government of India in Male and construction of the Composite Training Centre for the Maldives National Defense Force (MNDF).[28] Even in realm of tourism, it has been observed that there have been efforts to improve people to people contacts by way of increased air connectivity.

The number of tourist to the island states is increasing tremendously in the last few years (33000 people from India visited Maldives in 2014).

India, Sri Lanka, Maldives: A Way Forward through Trilateralism

India's engagement with Sri Lanka and Maldives is currently operated mostly through bilateral route, especially in the realm of trade and developmental initiatives. Such bilateral engagements which are on the rise, is likely to be enhanced through trilateralism as envisaged in maritime security trilateralism which came into existence recently (2014). Indeed, as far as trilateralism involving these three countries is concerned (in the sphere of economy), it is at a nascent state. However, it is often stated that India has a huge role to play in Maldives and Sri Lanka through trilateral arrangements wherein India can contribute to promote livelihood security and macro-economic stability. Apart from providing coastal EEZ surveillance, India can play a vital role in mitigating maritime pollution, climate change within a multi-lateral framework. Probably, India can also incorporate Mauritius and Seychelles in this framework.[29] The essence of this stream of argument is that India-Maldives-Sri Lanka Maritime Security Trilaterlaism should move beyond security centric focus to cooperate on non-traditional security issues such as environment, livelihoods and so on (while protecting security interests). Another aspect of trilateralism is that these three countries can promote 'Blue Economy'.[30] This particular idea has the potential to take care of the welfare of the people of Indian Ocean region in all the aspects such as providing a boost to national economies, sustenance of livelihoods, climate change mitigation, interconnecting economies at the regional level and so on. In a way, this human security centric approach will enhance multilateralism/trilateralism involving India, Sri Lanka and Maldives. India can also extend cooperation to address issues of climate change, which India can facilitate through its environmental and scientific institutions. Similarly, India can expand the operation of India's private sector since India has government centric approach at present.

There are several streams of arguments supporting the promotion of Trilateralism involving India, Sri Lanka and Maldives. For instance, prominent Indian Ocean observers such as P.K Ghosh argue that at the subterraneous level, the arrangement (trilateralism) will partly offset the growing influence of China and Pakistan in the regional dynamics. Most significantly, he further argues that, the arrangement will provide India with the option to utilize and foster forward bases (notional or real) in the entire region if the need arises.[31]India's role in safeguarding the maritime security, sovereignty and integrity is noteworthy. Accordingly, the latest trilateral agreement enables India to continue its role in the region to patrol and safeguard the Exclusive Economic Zones (EEZs) of its southern neighbours. Some of the aspects of the agreement specifically are to keep the Indian Navy and its security apparatus of being informed and updated about its southern neighbourhood, thereby avoiding any exigency of being surprised by adverse developments in its vicinity.[32] At a broader level, if the arrangement of Trilateralism works out, it has the potential to address common issues of the people of three countries, especially in the realm of economy, environment, in addition to the security of the region. Once such sub regional initiative through 'trilateralism succeeds, it would go a long way in strengthening over all regionalism in South Asia.

Conclusion

The dismantling of Cold War binaries at the global level, along with rapid expansion of the processes of globalisation has had its effects on the foreign and regional policies of states across the world. Regionalism has become a priority in the foreign policies of states. To offset the adverse effects of globalisation and extracting benefits out of integrated regional trade, many new regional blocs were created and existing ones assumed greater significance. States such as India was no exception to this trend. India, along with other states from South Asia and Indian Ocean weaved several integration groupings, out which the most prominent one is SAARC. Though provided several benefits, SAARC was caught up in several conflicts, mostly centring on bilateral issues. In such a scenario, India began to look for alternatives as evidenced from its efforts to cobble sub-regional groupings. Sub regional grouping through trilateralism has become a new focus in the regional strategies of South Asian states such as India. Some of these sub regional/trilateral initiatives are in the sphere of economy and security/strategy. Currently, India is involved Sri Lanka and Maldives in a trilateral framework on maritime security while economic relations are primarily operationalized through bilateral routes, which shows an upward mobility. At the same time an increasing realisation acknowledged by these countries is that trilateralism in economy, environmental and energy can provide added benefits to these states in a collective framework. Therefore, India's involvement with Sri Lanka and Maldives through trilateralism has the potential to emerge as a major practise in the near future.

Table - 1

Annexure 1 Indo-Sri Lankan Trade since 2010 (in Rs lakhs)

S. No	Year	2010-2011	2011-2012	2012-13	2013-14	2014-15
1	EXPORT	1595089.35	2095145.80	2168769.33	2764366.96	4103801.13
2	%Growth		31.35	3.51	27.46	48.45
3	India's Total Export	113696426.38	146595939.96	163431828.96	190501108.86	189634841.76
4	% Growth		28.94	11.48	16.56	-0.45
5	% Share	1.40	1.43	1.33	1.45	2.16
6	IMPORT	227873.44	303660.43	340419.73	406445.16	464275.90
7	% Growth		33.26	12.11	19.40	14.23
8	India's Total Import	168346695.57	234546324.45	266916195.69	271543390.74	273708657.84
9	% Growth		39.32	13.80	1.73	0.80
10	% Share	0.14	0.13	0.13	0.15	0.17
11	TOTAL TRADE	1822962.79	2398806.23	2509189.05	3170812.12	4568077.03
12	% Growth		31.59	4.60	26.37	44.07
13	India's Total Trade	282043121.96	381142264.41	430348024.65	462044499.60	463343499.59

S. No	Year	2010-2011	2011-2012	2012-13	2013-14	2014-15
14	% Growth		35.14	12.91	7.37	0.28
15	% Share	0.65	0.63	0.58	0.69	0.99
16	TRADE BALANCE	1367215.91	1791485.37	1828349.60	2357921.80	3639525.22
17	India's Trade Balance	-54650269.19	-87950384.49	-103484366.72	-81042281.88	-84073816.08

Note: Since 2006-07, Petroleum figures are being computed from Import Daily Returns (DTRs) to generate country-wise/port-wise tables. Upto 2005-06 consolidated petroleum import figures were being received from the Petroleum Ministry

Source: EXIM Bank, Department of Commerce, Government of India, http://commerce.nic.in/eidb/ (accessed on 1 October 2015).

Table - 2

Annexure 2 Indo-Maldives Trade since 2010 (in Rs lakhs)

S. No	Year	2010-2011	2011-2012	2012-13	2013-14	2014-15
1	EXPORT	45554.05	59778.57	66609.97	64298.93	93314.67
2	%Growth		31.23	11.43	-3.47	45.13
3	India's Total Export	113696426.38	146595939.96	163431828.96	190501108.86	189634841.76
4	% Growth		28.94	11.48	16.56	-0.45
5	% Share	0.04	0.04	0.04	0.03	0.05
6	IMPORT	14543.27	8742.37	3422.17	2391.02	2648.42
7	% Growth		-39.89	-60.86	-30.13	10.77
8	India's Total Import	168346695.57	234546324.45	266916195.69	271543390.74	273708657.84
9	% Growth		39.32	13.80	1.73	0.80
10	% Share	0.01	0.00	0.00	0.00	0.00
11	TOTAL TRADE	60097.32	68520.94	70032.14	66689.95	95963.09
12	% Growth		14.02	2.21	-4.77	43.89
13	India's Total Trade	282043121.96	381142264.41	430348024.65	462044499.60	463343499.59

S. No	Year	2010-2011	2011-2012	2012-13	2013-14	2014-15
14	% Growth		35.14	12.91	7.37	0.28
15	% Share	0.02	0.02	0.02	0.01	0.02
16	TRADE BALANCE	31010.78	51036.19	63187.80	61907.90	90666.25
17	India's Trade Balance	-54650269.19	-87950384.49	-103484366.72	-81.04281.88	-84073816.08

Note: Since 2006-07, Petroleum figures are being computed from Import Daily Returns (DTRs) to generate country-wise/port-wise tables. Upto 2005-06 consolidated petroleum import figures were being received from the Petroleum Ministry

Source: EXIM Bank, Department of Commerce, Government of India, http://commerce.nic.in/eidb/ (accessed on 1 October 2015).

Endnotes

1 Trilateralism in international relations generally refers to a policy or practice of maintaining relations and cooperation between three countries/states.

2 S, Shaji. 2007. 'India's Foreign Policy: A Study of Changing Trends Since 1990s', Unpublished Ph.D. Dissertation, University of Hyderabad.

3 Mohan C, Raja. 2003. *Crossing the Rubicon: The Shaping of India's New Foreign Policy*. New Delhi: Viking India.

4 The Look East Policy was also a consequence to the restructuring of its domestic economy under framework of economic reforms which was commenced in 1991 in India. At the same time, the 'Look East' policy of India assumed greater significance in the period. The scope and density of relations between India and the 10-member Association of South East Asian Nations (ASEAN) has been steadily growing.

5 Harshe, Rajen. 2001. 'Globalisation and Changing Notions/Practices of Boundaries in International Relations'. Unpublished Paper, presented in International Seminar on *International Relations and Globalisation: Indo-Russian Perspective*, at University of Hyderabad, January 23-24.

6 World Bank, 2015. 'Regional Integration in South Asia', Policy Brief, http://www.worldbank.org/en/ region/sar/brief/south-asia-regional-integration (accessed on 1 December 2015).

7 Dixit, J.N. 2003. 'Prospects of South Asian Cooperation in the Transformed World-Post 11 September', *South Asian Survey*, 10 (1): 43 - 55.

8 Harshe, Rajen. 1999. 'South Asian Regional Co-operation: Problems and Prospects', *Economic and Political Weekly* 34(18):1100-1105.

9 Mohan, C Raja. 2004. 'A Foreign Policy for the East', *The Hindu*, July 16.

10 Ramaswamy, Sridhar.2015. 'A Boost to Sub-Regionalism in South Asia', June 15, http://thediplomat.com/2015/06/a-boost-to-sub-regionalism-in-south-asia/ (accessed on 2 December 2015).

11 A . Michael. 2013. *India's Foreign Policy and Regional Multilateralism*. London: Palgrave Macmillan. p.92.

12 Kumar, Amit. 2015. 'BBIN MVA: Embracing New regionalism in South Asia', July 15, *Indian Council of World Affairs*, www.icwa.in/pdfs/PB/2014/BBINMVAPB09072015.pd(accessed on 31 November 2015).

13 News Report .2015. 'Will not allow Chinese military bases: Maldives assures India', *The Hindu*, July 24.

14 Kondapalli, Srikanth. 2014. 'Maritime Silk Route: Increasing Chinese inroads into Maldives' Institute *of Peace and Conflict Studies, New Delhi*, http://www.ipcs.org/article/china/maritime-silk-road-increasing-chinese-inroads-into-the-maldives-4735.html (accessed on 25 November 2015).

15 Ibid

16 Variyar, Mugdha.2015. 'Chinese 'Land Grab' in Maldives: How India Can Counter Beijing's Expanding Sphere of Influence', *International Business Times*, July 27.

17 Srinivasan, Meera. 2015. 'Sri Lanka keen on Indian Investment', *The Hindu*, March 6.

18 Information available in website of Sri Lankan Mission, http://www.mumbai.mission.gov.lk/index.php/trade/indo-lanka-trade-relations (accessed on 3 December 2015)

19 Ibid

20 'Ministry of External Affairs Portal', *Government of India*, http://mea.gov.in/Portal/ForeignRelation/Maldives_May_2014_.pdf (accessed on 12 November 2015).

21 Ibid

22 Ministry of External Affairs Data, cited in Gupta, Arvind. 2014. 'India and Maldives: Ties must be consolidated', *New Delhi: IDSA Policy Briefs, IDSA*.

23 Panda, Ankit. 2015. 'India's Maldivian Headache', *The Diplomat*, February 26.

24 For details see, http://www.gktoday.in/india-maldives-bilateral-relations/ (accessed on 25 November 2015).

25 Banerjee, Soma and Sruthijith K. K. 2012. 'GMR-Maldives Spat: Bali lateral Relations with Maldives under Review', *Economic Times*, December 5.

26 The reasons for such a drastic decline need to be probed further.

27 Gupta, Arvind. 2015. 'India-Maldives Ties should be consolidated', New Delhi: Policy Brief, IDSA.

28 Ministry of External Affairs. 2014. 'Joint Statement by the Prime Minister of India and the President of Maldives, http://www.mea.gov.in/bilateraldocuments. htm?dtl/22706/Joint+Statement+on+the+occasion+of+ the+State+Visit+of+P resident+of+Maldives+to+India (accessed on 1 December 2015).

29 Kumar, Vikas.2015. 'India-Maldives Greater Engagements Needed', *Future Directions International*, http://www.futuredirections.org.au/files/ Associate%20Papers/2015/FDI_Associate_Paper_-_India_and_the_ Maldives.pdf (accessed on 1 December 2015).

30 The Blue Economy is envisaged as the integration of Ocean Economy development with the principles of social inclusion, environmental sustainability and innovative, dynamic business models. It is founded upon a systems approach, wherein renewable and organic inputs are fed into sustainably designed systems to fuel "blue growth". Such "blue growth" addresses the problems of resource scarcity and waste disposal, while delivering sustainable development that enhances human welfare in a holistic manner. (Gist of ideas on "Blue Economy", projected by Indian Ocean Rim Association (IORA). For further details see, http://www.iora.net/blue-economy/blue-economy.aspx (accessed 2 December 2015)

31 Ghosh, P.K. 2014. 'Maritime Security Trilateralism: India, Sri Lanka and the Maldives', *Strategic Analysis*, 38(3): 283-288.

32 Karthikeyan, T.C. 2013. 'India, Sri Lanka and Maldives: Regaining India's Strategic Space', *IPCS Debates*, No:4078, July 13.

Chapter 6

Politics among the South Asian Troika: India, Sri Lanka and Maldives

T.C.Karthikheyan

Introduction

In the South Asian context, Sri Lanka and Maldives are situated in the vantage points with strategic importance. Historically, Sri Lanka has strong ethnic and socio-cultural ties with India. It was under India's influence for a long time and after its independence, it slowly started to assert its own autonomy to an extent. Consequently, it has as voted against India in international forums on many occasions, sometimes supporting Pakistan. Though, Sri Lanka remained a friendly state for India generally, the relationship between the two witnessed a series of a strained relationship. The first such incidence was the disfranchisement of upcountry Tamils in the 1950s, then the 1987 Indo-Sri Lankan accord which the Sri Lankan leadership thought that India forced such an agreement on it and the resulting Indian Peace Keeping Force intervention in Sri Lanka. Lately, after the Fourth Eelam War and the dismantling of the LTTE, the Rajapaksa regime became closer with China and compromising India's interests and concerns at times.

Maldives is a beautiful nation with more than just pristine beaches and cocktail venues. It also has a prominent place as a strategic state in the scheme of things in the South Asian context. Maldives had never been a part of any military alliance, and there were reports that the erstwhile USSR was ready to pay billions of dollars for a strategic post in one of the Maldivian islands. Maldives' foreign policy is basically driven by its dependency on other nations compelled by geographic structure, lack of natural resources and other economic disadvantages. Maldives gaining more important aspect of foreign policy making with regard to other states in the region is to do with the looming threat of terrorism in the region. This can be aptly recognised with the threats on the formation of Al Qaeda for the Indian subcontinent and possibility of Pakistan's ISI using radicalised Maldivians against India.

There are three main objectives for this paper. They are:

- To analyse the nature of political engagements between India, Sri Lanka & the Maldives (mostly bilateral in nature).

- To look into the levels & facets of political engagements & its implications on their mutual relationships.

- To evaluate the involvement of extra-regional powers & its repercussions.

This paper consists of three parts that are as follows;

- First part looks into the India- Sri Lanka relations

- Second part looks into India – Maldives relations

- Third part analysis the role of extra-regional powers' and their engagements in the region.

Indian Ocean Region

For any kind of analysis on the South Asian particularly if it involves India, Sri Lanka and Maldives, it is imperative to look into the importance of the Indian Ocean Region (IOR) for this region. IOR has exceptional economic, political and strategic significance of not only the countries in the region but also for the countries that have their vital commercial interests in the IOR. Emerging competition between the extra-regional powers in the region is becoming evident and plays an important role. The SOFA (Status Of Forces Agreement) agreement that was supposed to be signed between USA and Maldives reiterates this point. The backdrop of recent developments in piracy and seaborne terrorism the importance of the region became stronger. Therefore, it has become important to secure the uninhabited island territories in the region that could be used by the terrorists. Consequently, it becomes imperative for India to address and to evolve a cooperative mechanism with Sri Lanka and Maldives playing as important cogs in the polity and security of the region.

India – Sri Lanka Relations

Both these countries have historical linkages for centuries but failed to yield good political relationship due to the clash of priorities, personalities and political necessities. The problem in the equal treatment of Tamils right from the 1950s and the personality clash between Rajiv Gandhi and Jayawardene are such cases. The bigger problem emerged during the 1980s when the 1983 riots broke down in Sri Lanka against the Tamils. This took a violent retaliation by Tamil youths and there emerged many numbers of liberation outfits and LTTE was one among them. It is a known fact that India played a major role in training the LTTE and financial supports were given by the people of Tamil Nadu. One of the major instances of direct confrontation between the two was the time when the Sri Lankan government imposed an economic blockade of the Tamils living in the Northern and Eastern part of Sri Lanka. This necessitated India to drop food and essential medicines by air and sea in those parts of Sri Lanka without the permission of the Government of Sri Lanka.

Then came one of the major political outcome between the two when the leaders signed the 1987 Indo-Lanka Accord, that required LTTE to drop and surrender their weapons on the basis of some promises made by India and Sri Lanka, and also to find a lasting solution to the ethnic problem by amending the Sri Lankan Constitution that is popularly known as 13th Amendment. But things didn't work as intended. LTTE sensed that they are corned without making enough progress for the ethnic problem and they didn't surrender their weapons and continued their armed struggle. Meanwhile, some local outfits also protested against India saying India is behaving as a big brother and has pushed the 1987 accord on Sri Lankan people without their interest. It was at this time India sent its Indian Peace Keeping Force (IPKF). It is a peculiar situation in the South Asian history, where the force that went to uphold peace, security and stability, eventually ended up fighting a foreign guerrilla force in a foreign land. There were many reports that's has recorded the breach of protocol and its mandate by the Indian Army causing loss of life, prestige ad honour of the Tamils in Sri Lanka. In a twist of sequences, there were also reports that Premadasa authorized a clandestine operation to supply arms to LTTE to fight IPKF at that time. With all these political baggage, the India – Sri Lanka Free Trade Agreement was the only visible successful component of bilateral relationship at that time as a result of the political determination.

Ever since the assassination of the former Prime Minister Rajiv Gandhi in 1991 by the LTTE, India did not take much of an interest in the politics and relationship with the island nation. There was a bilateral relationship only at the paper and formal levels. Real engagements were not there and there was a kind of policy vacuum in India's policy with regard to Sri Lanka during that time. This obviously gave other extra-regional players a scope to strengthen their relationship with the island nation and this was aptly used by China with its growing economic might during the 1990s that gradually helped increasing its influence there. China got its influence and engaged vigorously with Sri Lanka during the decade of the 2000s. The domestic political compulsions emanating from the state of Tamil Nadu was also not helpful in mending India's relationship with Sri Lanka, as Tamil Nadu leaders were constantly not satisfied with the functioning of the Sri Lankan government and the non-fulfillment of its promises towards the Tamil question. Norway also took over the role of facilitator in the peace process during the 1990s and till the early 2000s between the Sri Lankan government and the LTTE and this was also supported by India.

The final Fourth Eelam War that resulted in the decimation of the LTTE and the killing of their prominent leaders gave a new found assertiveness from the leaders of Sri Lankan government. This was followed by some political expediency by then President Rajapaksa and its regime that became closer with China with lesser regard to India's security concerns and economic interests. Rajapaksa used the Chinese card to its fullest advantage even at huge costs (Chinese loans were given to Sri Lanka at higher interest rates). His government also indulged in relocating Sinhalese population in the Tamil areas and also by militarising the Tamil areas even after the war ended. This resulted in a failure to restore the trust among Tamils, which was also reflected by the Indian government and its leaders and thereby widening the mistrust between the two nations.

Ray of Hope and Optimism

The latest presidential elections that held in 2015 has brought a new ray of hope and optimism in the relationship between the two countries, as there is a new leadership at the helm in Sri Lanka that has defeated the former President Rajapaksa. There is also a veteran Prime Minister Ranil Wickramasinghe in office there that has helped infuse fresh thinking on both the sides. In fact, India's RAW (Research and Analysis Wing) was accused by certain sections of Rajapaksa supporters of interference to bring down the Rajapaksa regime. The first visit of both the new President and Prime Minister of Sri Lanka has resulted in normalisation and balancing act by Sri Lanka with priority for India. This was appropriately reciprocated by the Indian Prime Minister Modi with his Buddhism diplomacy where he visited sacred places of Buddhist worships in Sri Lanka and also by visiting Anuradhapura, Talaimannar and Jaffna.

Persisting Irritants

Even, after all, these cordial developments, there still exists some irritants in the Indo-Lanka bilateral relationships. The fishermen problem is a daily concern for both the nations where the fishermen from India cross the international border and venture into the Sri Lankan waters. This was mainly due to the transfer of the Kacha Theevu – an Indian island territory that was transferred to Sri Lanka in the 1970s even after the opposition from the leaders and people of Tamil Nadu. Now the people of Tamil Nadu wants that island territory back to India and the Chief Ministers of the state has also written to the Indian President and Prime Minister time and again in this regard. Without a full working cooperation from Tamil Nadu political leadership, a lasting solution to this issue is not at all possible. This issue also created some aberrations during the general elections in Sri Lanka where a controversial statement was made by one of the prime ministerial candidate Rani, which offended the Indian fishermen from Tamil Nadu. The next persistent and unavoidable issue between the two is the case for devolution of the northern and eastern parts of Sri Lanka like that exists in the other parts of the island nation. India's push for devolution and the implementation of the 13th amendment has been a major irritant between the two. The ensuing assembly elections to be held in 2016 in the state of Tamil Nadu will see high octane political contestation between different political parties with regard to the welfare of the Sri Lankan Tamils and the role of Indian government in ensuring peace, dignity, stability and security for the Tamils in Sri Lanka.

India –Maldives Relations

The nature of the relationship between India and Maldives were always cordial. Maldives is mostly dependent on India and Sri Lanka for its day to day existence mainly due to its vulnerability with regard to the lack of resources and wealth. India and Maldives are sensitive towards each others' security needs mainly due to tension-free socio-historical settings and interaction. The relationship between the two countries cannot be compartmentalised solely on political relationships as everything is intertwined. Decision at social and economic spheres will definitely have its impact in the political sphere too. Global warming and the rising Sea level affect the existence of Maldives as a nation and eventual disappearance within the next 100 years as envisaged by a UN expert group of climate change. Accordingly, Maldives planned a "sovereign fund" in 2008 to buy a home and land for its people in India – it's a testimony to its faith and confidence on its big neighbor - and the cordial relationship it has developed with its big neighbour without the problem of "Indophobia".

India's Assistance

India has assisted Maldives in many critical situations in its long friendship with the atoll nation. It was on 3rd November 1988, India undertook "Operation Cactus" – a combined operation of Indian Navy and Indian Air Force to safeguard the sovereignty of Maldives. India extended its military help immediately when some mercenaries from Sri Lanka aided by wealthy Maldivian businessman from Sri Lanka threatened to overtake the Maldives by capturing the President and other military personnel. But the timely intervention by the Indian armed forces, not only reinstated the legitimate government of Maldives in the hands of Maldivians but also strengthened its faith and friendship with India.

India sent its coast guard and Navy for rescue and relief operations immediately after the Indian Ocean Tsunami that affected the south Asian countries on 26th December 2004. It was a great gesture by India since India itself was severely affected by that tsunami. India showed its concern towards Maldives in that instance and its capability was also visible to the world powers during the times of disasters. India also provided monetary and infrastructural assistance for Maldives to overcome serious financial difficulties on account of the tsunami and related factors. Apart from this assistance, India has been playing a major part in Maldivian security like no other country. In fact, one of Indians long-standing close military engagement is with Maldives only. Bothe these states has a robust maritime cooperation in place that helps in providing military hardware, training of its security personnel and offering surveillance facilities in the Maldivian exclusive economic zones. India has also supported Maldives in many issues consistently including heath care. The biggest hospital in the country, Indira Gandhi Memorial Hospital located in the capital Male is a gift by India. All these assistance are not possible without the political understanding and engagements at the highest levels of the political rulers.

Political Engagements

Even if we could not compartmentalise many of the engagements between the two as purely political, there are few other instances that are political in nature. India's support for the democracy movement right from 2003-2004 is a case in point. India has continuously engaged with the democratic movement in Maldives to establish institutionalising the democratic process in the island nation. India has trained their election commission by inculcating skills and capabilities to conduct elections in the nation that is widely spread over among numerous islands. India is also sending its observers for every presidential and parliamentary election that are being held in Maldives. Another instance to be noted is that both the presidential candidates of the last election seeking India's cooperation and goodwill, thereby showing the political understanding and involvement of both the countries for mutual benefits.

Concerns

There have also been some concerns in the bilateral relations lately. All these started in February 2012 when a President Nasheed controversially removed from the power which he calls as "under duress" and a new President took over from him under military conditions. India immediately within hours recognised the new President leaving the reality of what happened actually. The new regime got closer with the China that was not expected by India. The Chinese card was played by the sections of Maldivian Politicians (lesson from Sri Lanka) and they also increased polarisation in domestic politics, combined with religious extremism. The major jolt in Indo-Maldives relationship in the recent times came when the Indian company GMR's $500 million airport development project in the Maldivian capital was cancelled due to domestic political conditions in Maldives. India condemned it strongly and the case was pursued at the international level. Other major concern arose when Nasheed took refuge in Indian High Commission in Male briefly against his arrest by the then Maldivian regime. But the timely involvement and diplomatic skills of the Indian diplomats solved the issue without major damage. The other major problem that has arisen between the two in recent times was the massive Chinese involvement in most of the spheres including economy, tourism, housing projects, etc. Currently, Maldives tries not to antagonize India, as India is capable of inflicting severe damage to its survival in terms of economy and military. In spite of that, without naming India, Maldivian leaders are also voicing their concerns about external interferences in its domestic issues. Indian Prime Minister Modi also left out Maldives at the last minute from his tour of IOR countries like Seychelles, Mauritius and Sri Lanka, when Nasheed was jailed.

Extra-Regional Powers' Engagements

Sri Lanka's engagements with extra-regional powers, particularly with China, witnessed a commendable increase during and after the fourth Eelam War. China supported Sri Lanka massively at the UNHRC on the investigation on Sri Lanka's Human rights violation and war crimes. John Kerry's visit to Sri Lanka, the first by a U.S. Secretary of State in 11 years, also recognizes the country's geopolitical importance in the current milieu. United State's interest in the region shall be gauged righty when they requested for a Status of Forces Agreement (SOFA) with Maldives, thereby gaining access for its military ships and forces to the islands of Maldives. China has also remarkably enhanced its presence in Maldives in a short period in many aspects particularly with its great influence on Maldives' economy via infrastructural projects and tourism sector. China is also looking forward to avenues and plans to invest massively in renewable energy and environmental security projects in Maldives. China's insistence on a new Maritime Silk Route in the IOR and the enthusiastic support given by Sri Lanka and Maldives is a concern for India's security.

Conclusion

India's concrete political engagement with Sri Lanka and Maldives helps in improving its capacity to defend its vital interests in the Indian Ocean, as well as to reinforce its regional strategic pre-eminence. India has to devise appropriate policies to keep other state's influence at a distance. India should also take that Sri Lanka and Maldives are not India's "shadow state" anymore and the enthusiasm showed by these two southern neighbours on the new maritime silk route is a case in point. The proposed CEPA (Comprehensive Economic Partnership Agreement) shall bring more positive engagements between these three countries. The current internal political dynamics in Maldives necessitates political prudence and intelligent maneuvering. Furthermore, India has to pin its hope on democracy and its dividends. It should also try to use its economic leverage to fulfill both the southern neighbours' needs in their developmental agenda. Whoever leads these countries politically, economic cooperation combined with political engagements only could strengthen ties in a mutually beneficial way. India should also take a serious note on Indian commitments on project costs that it has undertaken in those countries and deadlines for those projects should also be met promptly. India should also realise that whoever may form the government in Sri Lanka and Maldives and whoever may be the leader of those nations, pro-China lobby in Sri Lanka and Maldives is a reality that India has to contend with by any form.

References

Dikshit, Sandeep (2006) "India transfers naval ship to Maldives" http://www.hindu.com/2006/04/17/stories/2006041706371200.htm

Group Captain Bewoor, A.G., "Operation Cactus: Reminiscences" Available at http://www.bharat-rakshak.com/IAF/History/1988Cactus/Cactus01.html

Haidar, Suhasini (2015), "Knitting the India-Sri Lanka relationship closer". Accessed on August 13, 2015, http://www.thehindu.com/opinion/blogs/blog-suhasini-haidar/article6989225.ece

Kapila, Subhash, "India Defines Her Strategic Frontiers", *South Asia Analysis Group*, Paper No. 832, November 4, 2003, http://www.southasiaanalysis.org/%5Cpapers9%5Cpaper832.html

Khurana, G.S. (2004), "Maritime Security in the Indian Ocean: Convergence Plus Cooperation Equals Resonance", *Strategic Analysis,* Jul-Sep 28 (3): 411-426

Nataraj, Geethanjali and Sekhani, Richa (2015), "A new era for India–Sri Lanka relations?" Observer Research Foundation. Accessed on 7 September 2015. http://www.eastasiaforum.org/2015/03/07/a-new-era-for-india-sri-lanka-relations/

Pethiyagoda, Kadira (2015), "India v. China in Sri Lanka: Lessons for Rising Powers", Accessed on 11 August 2015. http://thediplomat.com/2015/05/india-v-china-in-sri-lanka-lessons-for-rising-powers/

Radhakrishnan, RK (2011), "Blake to visit Killinochi," The Hindu http://www.hindu.com/2011/05/01/stories/201105016491800 p.18

Ranasinghe, Sergei DeSilva (2011), "China-India rivalry in the Maldives", The Jakarta Post, 17 June 2011, http://www.thejakartapost.com/news/2011/06/17/china-india-rivalry-maldives.html

Sahadevan, P. (1999), "Maldives, in Security in South Asia," Banerjee, Dipankar, New Delhi: Manas Publications

The Hindu (2010), "'Huravee' handed over to Maldives after refit," http://www.thehindu.com/2010/02/12/stories/2010021253660200.htm

World Defence Network, "India bringing Maldives into its security net", Aug 13, 2009, http://www.defence.pk/forums/india-defence/31655-india-bringing-maldives-into-its-security-net.html

Chapter 7

Recent Political Developments in Sri Lanka

P.M. Heblikar

Introduction

2015 has been so far a remarkable year in Sri Lankan politics. It has witnessed a sea-change in the text and tenor not witnessed in contemporary times. The massive national upheaval resulting from the defeat of Mahinda Rajpaksa at the Presidential elections held in January 2015 and his party's loss at the Parliamentary elections in the August same year created a new political equation resulting in the emergence of a new troika comprising President Maithripala Sirisena (PMS), Prime Minister Ranil Wickremesinghe and former President Chandrika Kumaratunga Bandaranaike. This has been considered as well for the country. The Parliamentary elections confirmed the mood for reconciliation and an end to an era of uncertainty. The lessons from the Parliamentary elections are many and to ignore them would be at one's own peril. The compass has been set for a new course aimed to retrieve lost ground, to build on the mandate for reconciliation and to end the international isolation caused by controversial policies of the Mahinda Rajpaksa regime. It is remarkable that extremist parties especially the Jatika Hela Urumuya (JHU) have been marginalized. The Janatha Vimukthi Peramuna (JVP) too has lost its sheen, which is a far cry from yester years. The Tamil parties have been returned to Parliament in same numbers as in the past but may have lost their bargaining clout. The other remarkable aspect is that the two major political parties had to fight hard to retain relevance among their electorate and also to underline the fact that minorities could no longer be taken for granted. The previous government of Mahinda Rajpaksa paid for its shoddy treatment of the minorities. Two things are very clear that the two Sinhala major parties have realized it is time for reconciliation and that there is no place for rancor or ill-will. The cynosure is on President Maithripala Sirisena as to how he presides over the new mandate given to his coalition.

Reconciliation as new mantra

The appointment of Chandrika Kumaratunga as head of the national reconciliation task force was in right direction given her impeccable credentials on the ethnic issue. There is hope in the air for constitutional and political reforms in Sri Lanka. The appointment of eminent Tamil persons to significant positions in the cabinet, in the council of ministers, in the government as also is that of a civilian Governor for the Northern Province and a new Chief Secretary for the same province was evidence of the determination. By such pro-active appointments, the government has sent positive signals. These are precursors towards national reconciliation after decades of narrow communal politics. The current political environment is unprecedented and hopefully will mature as the country prepares for crucial parliamentary changes in next few months. It is interesting to note the absence of discordant notes in the media on current development.

Sri Lanka had taken a totally different trajectory during the nearly decade-long rule of Mahinda Rajpaksa. A rational assessment would reveal that the country was unprepared in several terms for a post-civil war scenario especially towards rapprochement, reconciliation, reconstruction and re-development. Internal compulsions and external pressure on sensitive matters witnessed a regression in Sri Lankan political and constitutional matters. The root cause of the several decades long civil-war was perhaps not addressed for several reasons. History will judge Rajpaksa on this issue, especially his failure to convert opportunities into reality. There is, however, no denying the fact that Mahindra Rajpaksa was the architect of the military victory over the LTTE. Equally so, the contribution of Ranil Wickremesinghe for bringing Liberation Tigers of Tamil Elam (LTTE) to a cease-fire in 2001 needs also to be highlighted in strategic terms. Many experts agree that the cease-fire had a direct and debilitating effect on the LTTE. The rest is history.

One important aspect to be noted is the emphasis on creation of a new Constitution for the country. There is general consensus on the need to refocus for the new statute book to be dynamic and address the aspirations of all sections of the community as also to bring in checks and balances to prevent misuse and abuse of powers. The incumbent government has ground swell support on this score. Sri Lanka has embarked on a new journey and therefore needs to leverage the coalition character of its government to the maximum benefit and to ensure that the window of two years will be put to effective use.

The results of the August 2015 Parliamentary elections are significant in view of the desire for writing a new statute book. Even though no single party obtained the requisite majority in Parliament, it strengthened the mandate for good governance and underlined the importance of reconciliation. Observers feel that the present government can muster two third in passing the constitutional reforms. This assumes some degree of urgency in view of the limited period of the national government of two years. Further, the election of R Sampanthan as Leader of Opposition has put the onus on the various Tamil parties and the Diaspora to weigh in on important reforms that await the country. The Tamil representatives have a unique responsibility to shape the future of their community as also to engage with the Sinhala majority and moderate their views on subjects of national importance. The Pro-Mahinda camp has been weakened to a large extent by the results of the two major electoral exercises and may be expected to lie low for some time. Any attempt to interrupt the new democratic process may not augur well. It has perhaps learnt its lessons especially in handling the emotional subjects that have held the country captive for well over the past 60 years. The government has not lost time and has moved quickly on the political and diplomatic front to garner international support for economic development and also to endure that the safety net will be available to meet the demands for wider enquiry into the civilian deaths during the closing days of the civil war.

Political situation after 2001

At the turn of the century, it was increasingly evident that both the government and the LTTE had arrived at a military stalemate. There was no sign of any political will, on both sides, to bring an end the conflict. Both sides were at each other throats. India too realized that a fresh initiative was necessary to bring some closure to the situation in Sri Lanka. This time around, India got it right.

A cease-fire between the Sri Lanka government (SLG) and the LTTE came into effect in 2001, which had been brokered by the Norwegians with the support of India. Ranil Wickremesinghe, the then Prime Minister, played a major role in this direction with a team of some senior political figures, bureaucrats and international support. The cease-fire became a game changer as future events have had shown. Both the LTTE and the SLG held several rounds of talks at different locations overseas. The Oslo declaration of December 2002 changed the narrative to a large extent especially when the LTTE delegation agreed to discuss its demands within the four walls of the constitution. Clearly, the LTTE delegation was at variance with the directives of the leadership, this led to realignments at subsequent talks. SLG rather Wickremesinghe had won the first battle. It was not easy for him to conduct his peace diplomacy especially with a hostile President Chandrika Kumaratunga making it difficult for him to function. It is commonly acknowledged that she was unhappy that the deal with the LTTE had been made behind her back with Wickremesinghe keeping his cards close to his chest. 2003 was a year of political challenge for Wickremesinghe as he had to contend with economic downturn, conduct his negotiations with the LTTE and stave off political challenges from Kumaratunga.

On the other hand, Velupillai Prabhakaran was confronting his demons in the form of Karuna, his chief military strategist. It was becoming increasingly clear that LTTE was headed for a split and that Prabhakaran and Karuna had all but fallen out on issues of strategy, politics and personalities. The ceasefire was taking its toll in many ways, desertions were on increase, defalcations of funds were on the increase and insubordination and indiscipline too were becoming rampant. The break came in early 2004, when Karuna officially broke away from the mother organization and a few weeks down the road received discrete government support.

The duration of the cease fire, though short lived, witnessed some important landmarks. The creation of the Sri Lanka Monitoring Mission (SLMM) was clearly a novel method of supervising the fragile cease-fire. This arrangement was unprecedented in international peace keeping operations; it was created outside the sanction of the UN Security. The relevant parties realized that India would have serious reservations to a UN force with a peace keeping mandate operating in Sri Lanka. From its national interest, India would have been averse to any UN involvement in Sri Lanka in the name of peace-keeping or cease-fire monitoring. The "blue hats" functioned under trying circumstances in the Northeast province. The role of Norway in the gamut of cease-fire and peace talks and subsequently in post tsunami relief operations in north-east province did not gain appreciation across the political rank and file. Its detractors suspected a pro-LTTE tilt. Norway lost its influence in the post 2004 parliamentary elections and subsequently sidelined and pushed out soon after Rajpaksa became the President. A detailed description of the Norwegian role in the entire process is available in a 220 page report published by the Oslo authorities. India's role association with the cease-fire has been highlighted in the report.

President Rajpaksa exploited the opportunity of dealing with a politically weakened LTTE, which had not fully recovered from the split of early 2004. It was a brilliant move. Two things must be flagged for information. The Sri Lanka military, especially in Jaffna peninsula, was reorganized by Gen. Fonseka taking every opportunity offered by the cease-fire. Observers credit Gen. Fonseka with turning the military into a mean fighting machine. The boot was clearly on the other foot. Secondly, Gen. Fonseka received a clear political mandate from President Rajpaksa in unequivocal terms to militarily defeat the LTTE. It must be said to the credit of Rajpaksa who stood firm in his objective and gave the military every support necessary to vanquish Prabhakaran. Vellupillai Prabhakaran had overestimated his ability to confront Colombo. He failed to read the determination of the new Colombo government to end the civil war. Media reports suggested that prior to and after the Presidential elections, Rajpaksa had sent out feelers to Prabhakaran to resume negotiations. Prabhakaran committed two tactical mistakes that caused his downfall. The first mistake was to convert the LTTE into a regular military force from a guerrilla organization. The second one was to prevent the Tamil civilian population in the northeast province from participating in the 2005 Presidential elections. He feared that groundswell support of Tamil in the northeast would give PM Wickremesinghe clear victory in Presidential elections, which would be detrimental to LTTE's cause and subsequently undermine his strategic plans. Prabhakaran was aware that the international safety net put into place by Ranil had indeed become very effective and Sri Lanka received support and assistance from wide range of countries.

The closing days of the LTTE has been remained mired in controversy especially the manner of violence and unprecedented civilian death. The horror stories refuse to go away; however, it appears that the new government of Maithripala Sirisena and Ranil Wickremesinghe has negotiated the international opinion towards a domestic enquiry on the matter. An interesting highlight to be considered is the opening of talks by the government with the Diaspora and creating opportunities for support and better understanding of the situation.

Reset compass for India

For the first time in many decades, India has a friendly government in Colombo following both the Presidential and Parliamentary elections in January and August, 2015 respectively. Among today's troika of influence, India seems to be in a comfortable position with them, which is a cause of immense satisfaction. Ranil has a better equation with the top policy makers in Delhi including the intelligence agencies. To his credit, he avoided the mistakes made by Mahinda Rajpaksa and Chandrika, who brought in the Pakistan and China factor to balance Indian influence. Though Ranil's first term of office, 2001-2004 was short lived, it made a significant impact on policy makers in Delhi. Importantly, he delivered on most of his pre-electoral promises made prior to the 2001 Parliamentary elections. This was unprecedented given the text and tenor of bilateral relations between both sides.

Seen from a geo-political perspective, it is for the first time in many decades that India will have a stable and friendly government in Colombo. In fact along with Bangladesh and Bhutan, Sri Lanka offers a relief from the tensions of the past and makes for a peaceful neighborhood. Ranil Wickremesinghe understands Indian concerns and will articulate his response suitably. India has to reach out to him and Sri Lanka with a clear and cogent policy. India has also to reach out to others as well so as to keep the consensus viable and acceptable.

Ethnic issues in the bilateral relations

It is important to analyze some key elements in India-Sri Lanka relations that have a profound effect on national politics of both countries. The roots of Sri Lanka's ethnic conflict originated during the British colonial rule, it simmered at the time when democratic institutions were being built in that country. The conflict emerged into prominence when London announced that power was to be handed over to a Parliamentary form of government elected by adult franchise. It was the view of the Tamil polity that the proposed Constitution was unsuited to meeting aspirations of the Tamil people. The creation of the Federal Party in 1948 was a defining movement and the resolution accompanying the declaration reflected the demands and objectives in unambiguous terms. This was interpreted as a claim for a separate Tamil state and linked federalism to separatism. This claim preceded developments even before Sinhala was declared to be the only official language in 1956. The Tamil United Liberation Front (TULF), a direct descendant of the Federal Party; other Tamil political parties except the All Ceylon Tamil Congress, began as off-shoots of TULF and remained at the forefront of political and militant activities. They are now represented in Parliament as also in the Provincial Councils in some form or the other. These parties had to endure the wrath of the LTTE and consequently functioned as Tamil National Alliance (TNA) under duress.

India-Sri Lanka relations moved in an uneven keel after 1948 by which time both countries had achieved independence, India in August 1947 and then Ceylon in February 1948. DS Senanayake (1947-52) and subsequently the United National Party (UNP) maintained close links with London and the Commonwealth. Senanayake's strategy for country's strategy post-Independence was based on the assumption that the most likely threat would come from India. In 1956-59, SWRD Bandarnaike, then Prime Minister, who was a member earlier of the Senanayake government, witnessed signing of defence agreements with Great Britain. Even so, diplomatic relations remained cordial at all times. From the time of independence till 1970s, the only outstanding issue which involved attention of both governments was the citizenship rights of the Tamil population – a legacy of the British colonial rule. India was then justifiably and legitimately concerned about the interests of the Indian Tamil population, especially of those who had opted to return to India and others who at that time were classified as "stateless". The issue received prominence and more Indian involvement following Mrs. Indira Gandhi's return to power in 1980. A noted Sri Lankan scholar assessed that Sri Lanka's geo-strategic location is a prime factor influencing its ethnic conflict. Its proximity to Tamil Nadu, home to over 60 million people, makes it even more difficult to manage the issue. Domestic pressures on the central government politicians in Tamil Nadu, especially during the coalition era, have added to the already sensitive situation. This was evident during the ten year rule of the Congress led United People's Alliance (UPA) government (2004-2014)though several central governments earlier had to contend with it.

The Indo-Sri Lanka Accord (ISLA-87) signed in July 1987 is an extra-ordinary document with substantial relevance even today. Dr. Kumar Rupasinghe's article entitled *Negotiating Peace in Sri Lanka: Efforts, Failures and Lessons* explains the impact of this accord ion the bilateral relations. Former India's National Security Advisor and Ambassador to Sri Lanka when the accord was signed wrote an article "Indian Involvement in Sri Lanka and the India-Sri Lanka Agreement of 1987 – A retrospective evaluation" explaining in detail about the applicability of the article. The Muslim community has been critical of the fact that over its non-inclusion in the agreement and the mood is captured by Dr. Uvais Ahmed in his article "A Muslim Perspective". Objectively speaking the Indo-Sri Lanka Agreement brought about far reaching changes in that country and was achieved against difficult political environment. The Thirteenth Amendment remains its central piece as also an item of emotional and political appeal. The ISLA-87 provided both countries with a mechanism to address national security concerns with a view to ensure long term stability in bilateral relations.

The ten year period of the Congress-led United Progressive Alliance rule (April 2004 to May 2014) witnessed a massive downturn in bilateral relations. There was a change in guard in Colombo with Ranil being voted out of office in the Parliamentary elections. The reins of power were back with Chandrika though she had to contend with Mahinda Rajpaksa as her Prime Minister. The equation Colombo enjoyed with Delhi during the time of the BJP led National Democratic Alliance changed remarkably. Ranil, in his time as the Prime Minister, had closely cultivated India and ensured that no new synergy was introduced into Sri Lanka foreign and security policy without consulting India. In doing so, he avoided giving space to both Pakistan and China, he also chose carefully to cultivate western governments without raising hackles in Delhi. To India's credit, it responded equally and supported him in his endeavors. Post-April 2004 witnessed the old Sri Lankan policy of pitting China and Pakistan against India. This received even more vitriol in the post-May 2009 military defeat of the LTTE. The compulsions of coalition politics in India during the ten years of the UPA rule had frittered away the advantages gained in the post-1999 period. This was seen mostly in India's immediate neighborhood. The problems in Sri Lanka and Maldives underlined the difficult foreign options for India.

The government of President Maitripala Sirisena has embarked on several confidence building measures in keeping with his election promises especially the desire to bring about Constitutional and political reforms. It has also to overcome the political mess left behind by predecessor administration of Rajpaksa, whose ten year reign in office had all but compromised the four pillars of Sri Lankan society. More "out of box" solutions are necessary to bring substance to Constitutional and other reforms. Several suggestions have been pro-offered in this direction including the need to create an Upper House of Parliament, mainly to give voice and representation to the provinces. A bi-cameral Parliament is both a constitutional and political necessity for the country. Another recommendation is to the creation of Vice-President's post is important to strengthen the existing system. These should, inter-alia, be a reason to make Sri Lanka adopt a secular outlook without compromising on its state policy. The post of the Vice-President is an important expression in this direction.

An important section of analysts underlines the need to fully implement the XIII amendment, the delay has brought into its wake several permutations and combinations. The original sense has been lost in the hurly burly of Sri Lanka's emotional politics. The XIII amendment is obviously an emotive issue that has divided the community along ethnic, religious and political lines. It is commonly acknowledged that lack of political consensus on its constitutional character especially the two sticking points relating to devolution of financial and police powers respectively to the provinces. This issue will be in the play list of reforms that is expected when the national leadership moves to write a new constitution. Constitutional experts and legal experts have indicated the possibility of bringing new synergy giving more powers to make the provinces stronger, which in turn will give the central government more authority on national management. President Sirisena has kept his promise of moving towards less executive presidency in favor of more powers to the political executive.

An Indian civil servant with long experience of dealing with India's neighbors states that unlike India, Sri Lanka's constabulary is controlled by Colombo in the matter of transfers, postings, deployments, recruitment and training of police rank and file. The other feature, according to him, is that, also unlike India, there is no buffer between the civil police and the military to handle serious threats to national security, law and order. According to him, the Special Task Force (STF) of Sri Lanka Police, which was created in early 80's, was to deal with LTTE insurgency in the Eastern Province and for security of Colombo. It was and is still an elite agency geared for counter-insurgency operations. The continuance of STF in its present form will perhaps remain unchanged. The need of the day, however, is to create a separate national police organization on the lines of India's Central Reserve Police Force (CRPF) to be stationed in the provinces for aid to civil power and other specially designated duties. It may be added that the STF played a major role in the rout of LTTE in the Eastern Province and in doing so relieved a bulk of the army for proactive operations in the north. India played a stellar role in enhancing the prowess of the STF especially in small team operations and in other areas also.

According to a former senior Indian Navy officer, the military in Sri Lanka today is in excess of requirements. Following demise of the LTTE, the threat to internal security has reduced. Gradual demobilization, carefully planned and executed, will release major chunk of funds to meet developmental requirements. One area of possible re-deployment of existing military is on UN Peace-Keeping duties on a rotational basis as was done few years ago. India with its rich experience of undertaking UN Peace Keeping duties can lend Sri Lanka a helping hand.

The role of two Indian Non-Government Organizations (NGO's) in carrying out Humanitarian Demining Operations in Sri Lanka during the period 2001-2012 must be highlighted. Both NGO's were raised from among ex-servicemen of the Indian Army. It involved removal of anti-personnel and anti-tank mines in Mannar and Vavuniya districts for resettlement of civilians in areas recovered by the Sri Lanka military activity from the LTTE. The trilateral activity, involving India, Norway and Sri Lanka, was a huge success. In the process, a large number of civilians, members of the military and other NGO's received training from them. The other contribution was in the field of Corporate Social Responsibility (CRS). The LTTE was taken aback by the arrival of the two NGO's in areas adjacent to its operational control but made no attempt either to intimidate or stop their activities. The cost of recovery was the lowest among the several agencies deployed in the activity. According to a media report, the Sri Lanka authorities offered this experience to Afghanistan for removal of mines in areas under government control.

Devolution of financial powers is a matter for serious introspection. There are many ways to resolve it. The way forward can be examined by a group of financial experts with the participation of the Central Bank of Sri Lanka and other stake holders. The possibility of a Finance Commission and a Parliamentary Committee to look at political aspects of the devolution of financial powers is another avenue for consideration.

Much work however remains to be done in closing the emotional gap on the vexed ethnic issue. While the implementation of the XIII amendment in its entirety is the common minimum expectation of the stakeholders, there is an urgent need to address the residual issues such as full rehabilitation of internally displaced persons, release of all those currently in government custody even after several years, investigation into disappearances of people and extra-judicial killings of persons during the last few years of the civil conflict. All this is not going to be easy and careful political actions are warranted. The role of stakeholders needs attention. The Tamil National Alliance (TNA) also needs to step up to the plate and display more maturity in making itself more relevant in national discourse. Though there is calm over the "victory" at Geneva on the issue of investigation, this process is fraught with risks. After all, the open finger pointing at those in power at the last weeks of the civil war may not happen for several reasons, it is quite possible that the burden will perhaps be carried by junior functionaries. The Sinhala sentiments will play a major role in any outcome.

A school of thought opines that the India-Sri Lanka Agreement 1987 has a major role even today in all aspects of bilateral relations. Due to the rough and tumble of national politics in Sri lanka, its implementation was more in breach and practice. According to media reports there have been attempts in the past to dilute its efficacy by getting foreign companies to undertake repairs at the Trincomalee harbor. Both sides may need to examine how to make this agreement workable in areas of mutual interest. The Comprehensive Economic Cooperation Program (CEP) continues to engage attention of respective sides and therefore needs early finalization. Briefly, Sri Lanka remains the largest beneficiary of India's development assistance as also its foremost trade partner. Time is now appropriate to redraw the contours of CEP and expand it into a Comprehensive Partnership Agreement (CPA).

The Jaffna peninsula requires greater developmental activities right from school and university education and skill development in social sector. There is the need to bring in qualified educators and teachers to bridge the existing gap, more investment in education technology, nurses for hospitals and first aid centers, IT, ICT, and service sector.

Military cooperation between both countries has been solid and there is every reason to believe that they will quicken and grow. This will be possible when military cooperation becomes part of the CPA. The CPA umbrella can also look at the fishermen's issue in the form of a mutually agreeable fisheries cooperation agreement.

Indian assistance to Sri Lanka in the post-civil war period has been outstanding especially in matters of reconstruction and redevelopment in the north and eastern provinces. This is especially in critical infrastructure sector. It will be recalled that at every possible emergency has stepped in to render assistance to Sri Lanka. The Indian rescue and relief efforts in the aftermath of the 2004 Tsunami is an example of rapid response of India which deployed its military and subsequently addressed other areas of immediate needs. Indian assistance came within hours of Rajpakasa's telephonic call to his Indian counterpart. In 2003, Indian military had provided assistance Sri Lanka to overcome the grim situation in Central province caused by incessant rains leading to massive damage to life and property.

A look at the Indian High Commission, Colombo's website lists the progress in bilateral relations as also sets out the development assistance provided in all sectors to that country. The stage is now set for resurgence in India-Sri Lanka relations. The coming few months will be crucial for it. This will depend on dynamic leadership in India and Sri Lanka to take things forward in desired direction. India will certainly look forward to regaining lost ground in Sri Lanka.

Newer Horizons

An analysis of recent developments in Sri Lanka would indicate that more time and effort is required to build further on the groundswell created by the coalition mantra and most importantly by the process of reconciliation. It will be slow and taxing process in dealing with emotive issues and personality based politics. One must not expect outstanding results in short period to time. A road map has been created and hopefully will be adhered by its proponents and others. Political stability and good governance is obviously the key to economic development. Ranil lost his campaign in 2004 due to inability to usher in strong economic reforms that would have brought some comfort to people, who had endured two decades of insurgency. This time around, the condition is favorable to him and is underwritten by western and other commitments of assistance. He has proved to be a better diplomat than Rajpaksa and has played his cards well. With India, too a new beginning has been made and hopefully, the mistakes of the past will be avoided and sincere efforts are made to redress the factors of destabilsation of bilateral relations.

References

Chand, Gurnam "Fishermen Issue between India and Sri Lanka", *Mainstream*, Vol. XLIX, No 13 10 October 2015, available at http://www.mainstreamweekly.net/article2634.html

Haidar, Suhasini (2015), "Knitting the India-Sri Lanka relationship closer". Accessed on August 13, 2015, http://www.thehindu.com/opinion/blogs/blog-suhasini-haidar/article6989225.ece

M.R. Narayan Swamy, *Inside an Elusive Mind*, Literate World, New Delhi, 2003.

Prabhakaran *Prabhakaran- a Leader for All Seasons*, International Federation of Tamils, 2004, Singapore.

Peebles, Patrick, *Historical Dictionary of Sri Lanka*, Rowman & Littlefield, Boulder, 2015

Radhakrishnan, RK (2011), "Blake to visit Killinochi," The Hindu http://www.hindu.com/2011/05/01/stories/201105016491800 p.18

Ranaweera, Lanka, Supannee Kaewsutthi Aung Win Tun Hathaichanoke Boonyarit Samerchai Poolsuwan and Patcharee Lertrit, "Mitochondrial DNA history of Sri Lankan ethnic people: their relations within the island and with the Indian subcontinental populations," *Journal of Human Genetics*, Vol. 59, 2014, pp. 28–36.

Ross, Russell R. and Andrea Matles Savada, *Sri Lanka: A Country Study*, Washington: GPO for the Library of Congress, 1988.

Silva, K.M. D', *A History of Sri Lanka*, New Delhi: Oxford University Press, 1981

Tyronne Fernando, Alien *Winds across Paradise: A New Look at Sri Lanka's Foreign Relations through the Ages*, Vikas Publishing House, 2002.

V. Suryanarayan, "Diversities and linkages in Sri Lanka," *The Hindu*, June 06, 2001, http://www.thehindu.com/2001/06/06/stories/05062524.htm

"Pawns of Peace – Evaluation of Norwegian peace efforts in Sri Lanka, 1997-2009," Chr. Michelsen Institute/School of Oriental and African Studies, University of London, September 2011, available at: http://www.oecd.org/countries/srilanka/49035074.pdf

"Sri Lanka: The Failure of the Peace Process" International Crisis Group, 28 November 2006, available at : http://www.crisisgroup.org/~/media/Files/asia/south-asia/sri-lanka/124_sri_lanka_the_failure_of_the_peace_process

Kumar Rupasinghe (ed), *Negotiating Peace in Sri Lanka: Efforts, Failures and Lessons*, London: International Alert. 1998

Dixit, J.N., "Indian Involvement in Sri Lanka and the Indo Sri Lanka Agreement: A Retrospective Evaluation in Negotiating Peace in Sri Lanka," International Alert Publication, February 1998

Chapter 8

Political Economy of Sub-regional Cooperation in South Asia: 'Looking South' policy of India

Anand P. Mavalankar

The evolution of regional cooperation in South Asia is marked by two-speed dynamic of cooperative relationships between and among South Asian states, beneath the larger South Asian regional cooperation edifice, marked by the establishment of the South Asian Association of Regional Cooperation (SAARC) in 1985. In contemporary times, the pattern of cooperative relationships among India, Sri Lanka and the Maldives is indicative of sub-regional cooperation among these states. Sri Lanka and the Maldives are two littoral states in the north Indian Ocean region that have engaged with India in both strategic and economic spheres. Given India's dependence on the waters of the Indian Ocean for undertaking her naval diplomacy, India's foreign policy-makers are concerned about India's relative neglect of its southern frontiers in early 21st century. Further, in view of the growing naval profile of China in the Indian Ocean region, India's foreign policy establishment has sought to deepen India's strategic and economic ties with Sri Lanka and the Maldives. The larger objective of the foreign policy-planners is to develop maritime infrastructure and other capabilities in the region.

In this essay, I shall endeavor to interpret India's cooperative efforts to build a strong foundation of Indo-Sri Lankan and Indo-Maldivian strategic and economic relations in contemporary times. Although Sri Lanka and the Maldives are member-states participating in the SAARC, their quest for engaging with India is distinctly special, due to Sri Lanka's proximity with India and India's close cultural ties with Maldives.

Sri Lanka is situated at the southernmost point of mainland Asia, the earliest travellers by sea found an indispensable port of call on the shores of this country. She is a pearl shaped tropical island of about 25,000 miles and 20.2 million people. Being situated off the southern tip – except the little Maldives which was administered as a dependency of Sri Lanka during the British colonial rule. Located some 200 miles southwest of Colombo, the capital of Sri Lanka, and comprising in the main of 12 coral islands with a total area of 175 square miles of a population around 0.4 million, which was administered as a dependency of Sri Lanka during the British colonial rule, offers no strategic advantage, but also poses no threat to it.[1] Not only was Sri Lanka rich in vegetation and other natural resources, it was also a heaven where sailing vessels were obliged to seek shelter while awaiting the trade winds for the onward journey. Much before Ceylon (now Sri Lanka) emerged as a sovereign nation-state in 1948, she had cultural, economic and social relations with 'Bharat' (of ancient and medieval ages and undivided British India) as a stateless society. The history of dynasties and kingdoms within the Sri Lankan society and their relations with 'Bharat' provides ample evidence in this regard[2]. While understanding and interpreting regional cooperation (and even sub-regional cooperation) with Sri Lanka in contemporary times, we need to bear this broad historical context in mind.

One of the major questions addressed in this essay relates to identifying relevant factors for accounting the political economy of sub-regional cooperation between Sri Lanka and India, especially since the 1990s. With the establishment of the SAARC in 1985, the institutional context of the cooperation among the South Asian states was established. Though it was a normative way of approaching cooperative/collaborative efforts among them, the ground realities of the broader South Asian landscape were not typically conducive among the participating member-states of the region.[3] It marked the institutional design of a regional organization, which expected the involvement of all South Asian states to take steps towards regional cooperation at one pre-determined given speed. Given the varying levels of economic development and uneven capacities of the states, there is greater realization in the past two decades[4] or so that for relatively 'smaller'[5] nation-states comprising the South Asian region, their quest for cooperation is predicated on the second speed, which is lower than the one envisaged in the SAARC's institutional arrangement.

India's policy of 'Looking South' reckons that Sri Lanka should figure prominently in the present stage of bilateral cooperation between the island state and India. With the end of the Civil War between the Liberation Tigers of Tamil Eelam (LTTE) and the Sri Lankan state earlier, there was recognition of the reality that India has to forge a multi-pronged approach to realize greater sub-regional cooperation with Sri Lanka. In this connection, C. Raja Mohan has identified one of the five foundations of India's foreign policy with her small neighbours, such as Sri Lanka and the Maldives. According to him, in the second decade of this millennium, the present National Democratic Alliance (NDA) government (that came to power in May, 2014) has to attend to India's national interest in terms of securing its borders, especially in the northern Indian Ocean region, which principally includes Sri Lanka. In view of the strains visible in recent past in India's relationship with Sri Lanka in regard to the Tamil question,[6] one notices steady loss of influence in the neighbouring Sri Lanka. To reclaim India's primacy in its relations with Sri Lanka, the present NDA government has given special attention to developing deeper economic ties between the governments and peoples of Sri Lanka and India.

Former Sri Lankan President, Mahendra Rajapakse's growing intimacy towards China was a crucial factor in reorienting India's 'Looking South' policy. As far as strategic affairs were concerned, China's assistance in developing the Hambantota Port and the frequent appearance of Chinese naval ships at the Colombo Port were significant developments. Clearly, the creeping expansion of the Chinese naval profile in the region has brought into sharper focus India's relative neglect of its southern borders with Sri Lanka. Further, the Chinese President, Xi Jin Ping's initiative to build a maritime silk road connecting the Pacific and Indian oceans and the support it has received from India's neighbours, has underscored the present Chinese Government's resolve to carve out its sphere of influence in the north Indian Ocean region.

In light of the above context, India's foreign policy establishment is compelled to look to its southern borders and strengthen its maritime strategic structure in the region. To begin with, the Indian government aims to respond to needs and requirements put forward by the Indian Navy to bolster its presence in the region. As a larger policy goal of the Indian strategic community, development of India's maritime infrastructure in the Indian Ocean region remains a predominant foreign policy objective. In the second decade of this century, India has expanded naval and maritime cooperation with the United States of America, Japan and Australia. As far as the Indian Ocean region is concerned, the Indian government has sought to consolidate its own traditional relationships with key Island-states like the Maldives, the Seychelles and Sri Lanka. India's engagement with Sri Lanka and the Maldives constitutes the central focus of this essay.

Another vital component to India's strategic ties with Sri Lanka relates to India's policy of 'Sagar Mala', a string of ports in the Indian Ocean region. The idea here is to create a maritime capability that would project India's power in the region. In the civilian maritime domain, one notices massive gap with China. Hence, the Indian foreign policy-planners have pursued the idea of installing a string of ports ('Sagar Mala') in the Indian Ocean. China's 'String of Pearls' in the Indian Ocean includes Hambantota Port in Sri Lanka (apart from Gwadar Port in Pakistan, projected as the forward base for the People's Liberation Army Navy [PLAN] of China, etc.). It is important to point out here that out of the top ten busiest container ports in the world today, China has seven of them.

China's maritime capabilities over the years have prompted her to project its military power outside its sphere of influence in the South China Sea.[7] China's military bases in the Indian Ocean have facilitated her to control critical choke points, and securing the sea lines of communication. China has further deployed blue water navy in the Indian Ocean region. In September, 2014, the Chinese President Xi Jinping's visit to Sri Lanka underscored China's role as a powerful extra-regional actor in the IOR.

In the past decade or so, China's efforts at forging economic cooperation with Sri Lanka and the Maldives have forced the Indian foreign policy establishment to rethink and intensify greater economic engagement of the Indian government with the Sri Lankan and Maldivian authorities. As regards the Maldives, one particular development in Indo-Maldives relations has uncovered certain flaws in India's public and private enterprises participation in the infrastructure sector of the Maldivian economy. In 2012, the government of Maldives cancelled the Male international airport contract with GMR and gave the contract of constructing the airport to a Chinese entity.[8]

Another aspect of India's relations with Sri Lanka and the Maldives relates to the role of ruling elites in facilitating or hampering sub-regional cooperation with the two island-states. Broadly speaking, there are two views on India's position and role vis-a-vis the successive governments in Colombo and Male. According to one school of thought, given the fund of goodwill and quality of government to government interaction as well as depth of people-to-people contacts, India's engagement with both countries has been consistently robust and historically time-tested or durable.[9] However, there is a second school of thought which takes the view that certain sections of the ruling elites in these two countries have played China card against India. According to this view, since China has opposed other states interfering in its internal affairs, Sri Lanka and the Maldives would prefer to endorse this Chinese position, while receiving economic assistance from the Chinese government or getting foreign direct investment from the Chinese companies. Given the 'politics-neutral' policy-stance of the Chinese government, the Sri Lankan and Maldivian authorities would prefer to do business with the Chinese leadership in bringing about economic transformation of their respective political economies.[10]

Given this line of thinking, the Indian foreign policy establishment has certain apprehension about the state and future direction of the political economy of sub-regional cooperation between India and Sri Lanka, as well as India and the Maldives. In more recent years, China's growing strategic access to critical locations in both Sri Lanka and the Maldives is noteworthy. China has intensified defence and maritime cooperation with these two countries.

Clearly, these developments have compelled the successive Indian governments to pursue a more vigorous sub-regional cooperation with Sri Lanka and the Maldives. Partly, it is meant to neutralise growing strategic and economic presence of the Chinese government and the Chinese companies. More positively, India has, of late, made efforts to utilise its naval strength and expand its maritime partnerships with other countries in the Indian Ocean region through bilateral, trilateral and multilateral means.[11] This has to be viewed in the backdrop of the Chinese naval submarines docking in Colombo, as well as the role of the Chinese navy in response to India's freshwater diplomacy in the Maldives.

To put it briefly, India has embarked upon rapid naval modernization of its assets /fleet to come to terms with rise of China as a formidable player in the Indian Ocean region. In the past decade or so, the successive Indian governments have given priority to engage more deeply and meaningfully with the successive Sri Lankan and Maldivian governments.

The visit of the Indian Prime Minister to Sri Lanka in March, 2015 (apart from visit to Seychelles and Mauritius) was aimed at realizing a vital part of the overall coherent maritime strategy. The political context of the visit merits elaboration. During the Presidency of Mahendra Rajapakse (2007-2014), his growing warmth towards China was largely due to China's assistance to Sri Lanka's strategic infrastructure. In particular, constructing the Hambantota Port by the Chinese government and frequent appearance of the Chinese naval ships at the Colombo port were indeed significant measures taken by the People's Republic of China. Further, the Sri Lankan President gave a whole-hearted support to the Chinese proposal on the maritime Silk Road during the Chinese President's visit to Colombo in September, 2014.

India's engagement with the Maldives

A small island-state of the Maldives, with a population of roughly 3,51,600 people (in 2014) with Gross Domestic Product (GDP) growth of around $3 billion in 2014, posted the GDP growth of 7.6% in 2014. Being a tropical nation with 26 coral atolls and hundreds of islands, it is blessed with beautiful beaches, blue lagoons and extensive reef. Its drivers of growth are tourism and fishing. Given its chronic fiscal deficit in the national budget, its development agenda relies greatly upon external Asian powers such as China and India, as well as international financial institutions such as the World Bank.

Another important dimension to the political economy of Maldives has been the ecological or environmental one. As regards the ecological status, the government of the Maldives has got a huge grant from the International Development Association (IDA), a soft-loan affiliate of the World Bank. This environmental project is aimed at enhancing the Maldives' capacity to effectively manage environmental risks and threats to fragile coral reefs as well as marine habitats resulting from tourism development, increased solid waste disposal, fisheries and global climate change.

The impact of climate change on the Maldives is indeed quite striking. Essentially, the Maldives is a low-lying archipelago with more territorial sea than land. It is faced with risks of intensifying weather events. As a consequence, sea level rises and thus poses severe existential threat to the very survival of the Maldives as a nation-state. Its future sea levels are projected to increase in the range of 10 to 100 centimeters by the year 2010, when it is feared that the entire country could be submerged.[12]

Given this grim scenario, on 6th April, 2010, a tripartite memorandum of understanding among the government of Maldives, European Union (EU) and International Bank for Reconstruction and Development (IBRD), worth $8.8 million was reached in Male to establish a new Trust Fund designed to build resilience to climate change in the Maldives. Its objectives are-(i) strengthening knowledge and leadership in the Government of the Maldives;(ii)generating adaptive capacity and climate resilience in key sectors through tangible pilot interventions; (iii) creating energy efficiency, especially renewable energy generation and distribution through low carbon options; and (iv) employing adaptation and mitigation interventions vis-a-vis climate change.

The scale of efforts for dealing with climate change in the Maldives is indeed quite huge. Out of total 1190 islands in 20 atolls, stretching over 900 km, the Maldives has 199 islands that are inhospitable. The highest point of land in the country is 2 meters or about 6 feet above sea level. The Maldives has, annually, about 500,000 tourists. Maldives atolls are ringed by the seventh largest coral reefs in the world and are among the richest in species diversity. The reefs host over 1900 species of fish, 167 coral species and 350 crustaceans.

The main engine of growth in the Maldives is nature-based tourism, which at present, accounts for roughly 70% of GDP. According to Richard Damania, World Bank's environmental economist, "Maldives' coral reefs, which protect it from storm surges and serve as the main attraction for the tourism-driven economy, are in danger of being damaged or destroyed by poorly handled waste disposal methods."[13]

The Maldives finds itself subject to negative impacts of climate change, and being a small state (in terms of economic capability). In the prevailing conditions, the Asian Development Bank (ADB) since 1978 has been a major development partner. It has dealt with projects pertaining to capacity building, public sector financial management, transport, energy and micro, small and medium size enterprises. The island-state has middle-income status despite its geographic constraints and contains risks as a small-island economy.

In this connection, it is worthwhile to point out that at the time of South Asia Sub-Regional Economic Cooperation Partnership Summit in Jaipur (India) on 16th January, 2015, the Vice-President for Operations at the ADB, Wencai Zhang, had stated that revitalizing South Asian Economic Cooperation in the midst of prevailing constraints was truly a formidable challenge. According to him, since the 1990s, South Asia as a region was growing at 6% per annum, and was second to East Asia in terms of overall growth. The crucial difference, though, is that the East Asian region is a deeply integrated one, while the South Asian region is currently least integrated in the world. In fact, South Asia's intra-regional merchandise trade share was 4.3% of its total merchandise trade in 2010, as compared to 5.5% for Central Asia, 26.4% for Association of Southeast Asian Nations (ASEAN) countries, 50% for NAFTA, and 71% for the European Union (EU).[14]

Currently, South Asia is 1/4th of world population, out of which 1/3 of the population is poor. It is estimated that one million new jobs are needed every month to reduce poverty in the region. Other challenges there are energy and food security, climate change and natural disasters. Given this big picture, policy-makers and opinion-leaders within the South Asian nations advocate Regional Cooperation and Integration (RCI).

Given the above state of affairs, it is imperative for countries like India to engage in sub-regional cooperation with Sri Lanka and the Maldives. The idea is to enhance cross-border physical connectivity, thereby reduce distance premiums and enable economies of scale. The whole point is to achieve trade facilitation by reducing trade costs and thus bring in efficiency. Consequently, market connectivity can leverage on physical connectivity in enterprises, which would promote regional and global value-chains. This whole thinking and actual implementation is characterized as South Asian Sub-Regional Economic Cooperation (SASEC) project that includes Bangladesh, Bhutan, India, Nepal, Sri Lanka and the Maldives.

The ADB's involvement, in this regard, relates to 33 investment projects, amounting to approximately 22 million dollars. One of the important objectives of the ADB is to create a robust transport infrastructure that would include dynamic multimodal transport networks that are connecting highways and sea-lanes across the South Asian region and beyond. The trade facilitation initiatives include modernization of customs, use of technology, reliability and track record of traders with incentives, the revised Kyoto conventional energy projects, and cross-border electricity transmission connectivity to promote long-run energy security.

The challenges to RCI include regional connectivity, the link between physical connectivity and basic infrastructures. Secondly, issues such as trade facilitation, regulatory process etc. are to be taken into account. The crucial aspect here is strong and well-connected transport infrastructure. Further, there has been lack of adequate ad reliable energy, so there is need to promote cross-border power trade and develop renewable energy options.

Another area for sub-regional cooperation is to evolve policy-regimes that are friendly (easy) to businessmen and investors. Here the prominent issues are number of documents that are needed to export, given that it takes longest time to export and the cost of exporting goods is too high.

Lastly, in the South Asian sub-region (as indicated above), the overwhelming priority is to create robust infrastructure and strong institutions, which are critical for generating more production and increasing trade among the countries. This can materialize in the short-run and in the long run if barriers to integration are reduced, regional infrastructure is strengthened, policies and regulations of countries are harmonized, regional energy security is enhanced and regional challenges of climate change and disaster preparedness are squarely met. The ADB has stated on 18th August,2015 that inadequate transport system can derail growth. The suggestion here is that connectivity among the atolls remains inadequate.[15]

Further, in a recent report entitled, Overcoming the Challenges of a small island state- country diagnostic study,[16] the ADB has recounted four constraints- (i) a transport network that is inadequate for enhancing connectivity among various atolls; (ii) a weak human capital and skills base; (iii) the chronic fiscal deficit and increasing debt burden; and (iv) the high cost of and limited access to finance especially for micro, small and medium investors.

Another vital dimension is that of security of the Maldives. With an eye on maritime threats, India finished the first phase of a security umbrella being build in Maldives with the installation of the third coastal radar system in the island state was complete. It would be beneficial for the Maldives National Forces to track ships and fishing boats, thus providing added security to the Exclusive Economic Zone (EEC) of the Maldives. The first radar was fitted at the southernmost Addu city's Gan Island in 2007. After the 2008 Mumbai terror attack, the Indian government took a serious note of maritime security and re-evaluated its strategic needs. After the assessment, second radar was installed in the northern island of Uligamu in 2012.[17]

In the previous two sections, we have provided certain facts and highlighted certain developments pertaining to India's sub-regional cooperation with India and Sri Lanka in contemporary times. The evolution of India's foreign policy was shaped by external developments as well as changes in India's domestic economic policy since 1991. With the dissolution of the Soviet Union in December, 1991 and end of the Cold War between the USA and the former Union of Soviet Socialist Republic (USSR) in 1989 paved the way for the post-cold war world order in which, at least in the 1990s, the pre-eminence of the USA as a hegemonic power in the post-cold war international political system was acknowledged by the major powers and other lesser powers as well. In the changed global order, India's diplomacy with the rest of the world had undergone change. On one hand, India was compelled to re-engage and recalibrate its stance with the USA and rethink the tenets of its policy of non-alignment with the superpowers and other major powers.[18] On the other hand, India had to recast its economic diplomacy in engaging with all major powers of the world in terms of exploring and expanding economic ties with major powers in Europe, Japan and the United States of America.[19]

At the same time, India was keen to promote greater cooperation with its South Asian neighbours, renewing strategic ties in Asia and the Indian Ocean region. Although the cold war strategic context of the international political system was no longer relevant in the post-cold war world order (beginning in the early 1990s), the normative approach and idealistic outlook underpinning the broader conception of 'non-alignment'[20] were still quite relevant and significant for conducting India's foreign policy in a conflict-ridden environment within the South Asian region.[21] In view of the political disputes and conflict between India and Pakistan at a bilateral level, the vision of the SAARC remained far-fetched for the member-states in the region. In such strategic environment, the Indian foreign policy-makers were keen to pursue sub-regional cooperation among India's neighbours in its southern frontiers, more specifically within the Indian Ocean region.

In the late 1990s, the 'Gujral Doctrine' highlighted the idea of 'positive unilateralism'[22]. It contains these elements- (i) the SAARC turned out to be dysfunctional, as its failures are rooted in geography and history of the countries associated with it; (ii) most of the regional trade is between India and its neighbours; (iii) the integrated economic space of the Indian sub-continent under the British Raj was broken up into several inward-looking markets of the newly-independent countries of India, Pakistan and Sri Lanka. These markets were subjected to economic reform under liberalization of the domestic economy and tides of economic globalisation across the planet earth. This created conditions for attempting regional integration among the South Asian states; and (iv) the two-speed SAARC was envisaged, wherein sub-regional cooperation was attempted in the interim stage.

In the big picture stated above, unilateral actions/policies by the Indian government for realizing sub-regional cooperation with Sri Lanka and the Maldives are in order. The first such unilateral initiative involves a SAARC satellite for use by its neighbours. Secondly, the Indian government should institute a policy whereby the Indian market should be opened for goods produced in the neighbouring countries, by reducing barriers to bilateral trade and allow trade facilitation. Thirdly, India should provide transit facilities for its neighbours, such as Sri Lanka and the Maldives. Fourthly, the Indian government should extend unilateral visa liberalization for the citizens of Sri Lanka and Maldives. Fifthly, the Indian government should extend financial facility for liberal lending to trans-border connectivity projects in the subcontinent.

Endnotes

1   Both Sri Lanka and Maldives have reasonably peaceful relations between two island-states. For a comprehensive treatment of this theme, see Urmila Phadnis, "Political Dynamics of Island States: A Comparative Study of Sri Lanka and Maldives", *IDSA Journal*, Vol.12, No.3, 1980, pp.305-322

2   For a detailed exposition of this point, see K.M. D' Silva, *A History of Sri Lanka*, New Delhi: Oxford University Press, 1981

3   This relates to the tension between the normative character of the SAARC project and the empirical nature of the actual ground-realities prevailing across the political landscape of the South Asian region, comprising distinct sovereign states. If one compares the region with the wider European region, the relatively compatible sovereign states of Europe and the forging of the European Union (EU) catch our attention. As regards South Asia, the geographical unity of the Indian subcontinent and India's natural geographical advantage have facilitated India's role as the regional security provider. Having shared cultural inheritance, India and Pakistan remain entangled in long-standing political dispute regarding Kashmir. Both countries face the similar challenge of eradicating poverty and raising the level of economic prosperity for all sections of their respective societies.

4   In the early 1990s, the emergence of the post-cold war world order fundamentally transformed the strategic environment for India. India's growing engagement and greater association with the United States of America in both economic and strategic realms enabled India to offer greater economic assistance to Sri Lanka and Maldives. Further, economic globalisation facilitated reduction of trade barriers between India and Sri Lanka, as well as between India and Maldives.

5   On the conceptual category of 'small state', see Sivananda Patnaik, "Small States in International Politics: A Case-Study of Foreign Policy of Sri Lanka (1948-1988)". Ph.D. Thesis, Department of Political Science, Faculty of Arts, the Maharaja Sayajirao Univesity of Baroda, Vadodara, March 2014, see especially chapter one, which deal with the critical examination of existing literature on the small state.

6   India's concerns with Tamil minority in Sri Lanka after the 2009 victory of the LTTE were reflected in India's foreign policy with Sri Lanka since 2009. Delhi's flipflops at Geneva in the UN debates on the human rights situation in Sri Lanka, the former Prime Minister's decision to skip visiting Colombo for the Commonwealth Summit in November, 2013 and the UPA government's

alleged ceding on a veto to Tamil Nadu over the country's foreign policy are some of the significant manifestations of India's foreign policy dilemma in dealing with the Tamil question in India's Sri Lanka policy.

7   Colombo's China relationship in the past decade or so has revealed new economic and strategic options available to Sri Lanka. China's relations with Sri Lanka is interpreted historically by various scholars. See Gamini Navaratne, *The Chinese Connexion.* Colombo: Sandesh News Agency, 1976. Also, see S.U. Kodikara, "Ceylon's Relations with Communist Countries, 1948-1966," *South Asian Studies,* Vo.2, No.2, 1967. Also, see Anuradha Muni, " Sri Lanka's China Policy: Major Trends", *South Asian Studies,* Vol.8, No.1, 1973.

8   It is not clear whether this decision was purely based on commercial reasons, or whether there were political interests involved therein.

9   Sri Lanka had access to a diversity of socio-cultural influences from the mainland of India. On this point, see M.D. Raghavan, *India in Ceylonese History, Society and Culture.* New Delhi: Asia Publishing House, 1969, revised edition. Also, see Urmila Phadnis, *Ethnicity and Nation-Building in South Asia.* New Delhi: Sage, 1990. Also, see S.D. Muni, *Pangs of Proximity: India and Sri Lanka's Ethnic Crisis.* New Delhi: Sage, 1993.

10 It seems there was convergence of views of governing elites of Sri Lanka and Maldives on this point with the Chinese leadership at that time.

11 Most Indian Ocean states had actively sought military support from one or the other external powers to counter presumed threats from their neighbours. To cement maritime partnerships with states like Sri Lanka, India had to bolster and deepen its naval strength. Over the past few decades, India has embarked on the path to rapid naval modernisation, expansion of civilian maritime infrastructure, the development of island territories, the capacity to undertake projects in other countries across the littoral and more vigourous assistance to other countries.

12 This refers to the environmental project granted by International Development Association, a soft-loan affiliate of the World Bank, to address the problem of environmental impact of climate change in Maldives

13 This was the expert opinion given by the economist concerned under the auspices of the World Bank.

14 Speech by ADB Vice-President for Operations Group 1 Wencai Zhang at the South Asia Subregional Economic Cooperation Partnership Summit on 16 January 2015 in Jaipur, India, available at: http://www.adb.org/news/speeches/

revitalizing-south-asia-economic-cooperation-enablers-midst-prevailing-constraints

15 This was noted by the Asian Development Bank in August, 2015.

16 This was a report by the ADB Report entitled, *Overcoming the challenges of a small island state – Country Diagnostic Study.*

17 See *Indian Express*, 27th August, 2015.

18 With the dissolution of the former Soviet Union in 1991, India was faced with a qualitatively different strategic environment in which she was compelled to engage with the United States of America in both strategic and economic spheres. Further, there was a historic shift in the Indian Ocean region with China emerging as a major naval power.

19 See C. Raja Mohan, *Modi's World: Expanding India's Sphere of Influence*, New Delhi, HarperCollins, 2015, P. 43-45.

20 For a detailed treatment of the broader conception of non-alignment, see A.P.Rana, *Imperatives of Non-Alignment: A Conceptual Study of India's Foreign Policy Strategy in the Nehru Period,*New Delhi, Macmillan, 1976.

21 It mainly relates to the problem of cross-border terrorism that has bedeviled Indo-Pak relations for the past two decades or so.

22 This doctrine was propounded by former Prime Minister I.K.Gujral in the late 1990s, which propounded the idea of positive unilateralism in India's Foreign Policy.

Chapter 9

Maritime Silk Route and the Role of Sri Lanka: Challenges and Opportunities for India

Jiss Tom Palelil

Introduction

Indian Ocean is the third largest oceanic division of the world covering 13.4% surface area of the earth. It is also home to huge amount of natural resource deposits. Most of the maritime trade in the region, particularly that of the Oceania and Asian continent, takes place through the sea routes which passes via the Indian Ocean[1]. It is this feature of Indian Ocean which makes it strategically as well as economically important to many countries, including India and China. The Indian Ocean and South Asian countries thus play a crucial role in shaping the economic, social and political feature of the world.

The Maritime Silk Route project (MSR) is a part and parcel of one of the signature foreign policy initiatives of Chinese president Xi Jinping. It is a $40 billion project to connect the 'dots' or the countries between China, Africa and Middle East. Maritime Silk Route, according to Beijing, is an initiative to deepen China's economic links with the West. This project was announced by the Chinese premier in 2013 during his visit to Indonesia. From then a lot of effort has been put up by Beijing to bring many countries, including India, into this project and to be a part of the resulting trade network. MSR is a part of 'One Belt, One Road' initiative of China to gain a superior position in the global economy by rejuvenating a parallel territorial Silk Road along with MSR. So far, over 50 countries, including

Sri Lanka, have agreed to be a part of this project and it is estimated that once completed, this project will have a potential of affecting the lives of around 4.4 billion people[2].

The New Maritime Silk Route

Maritime Silk Route (MSR) is one of the most ambitious projects proposed by Beijing to place itself as the global economic power. The MSR expects to reach Europe, starting from urban areas on China's south-eastern drift and utilizing an arrangement of connected ports and infrastructure projects. The proposed sea route starts in Fuzhou, China and goes by means of Vietnam, Indonesia, Bangladesh, India, Sri Lanka, the Maldives, and East Africa. Along the African coast, China proposes to create ports in Kenya, Djibouti, Tanzania, and Mozambique. The MSR would then proceed from the African coast into the Red Sea and through the Suez channel to the Mediterranean. Subsequent to passing Athens, the road ends in Venice, where it joins the territorial silk route.

Port and Infrastructure Development Proposals under MSR

Official claims of China state that so far, more than 50 countries from Asia, Africa and Europe have agreed to join the most ambitious initiative of China. Hungary became the first country from Europe to sign an agreement for joining the silk route. According to the Reuters estimation based on the data released by the World Bank, China's state backed financial institutions have already invested around $5 billion along the silk route in transport infrastructure over the past few years[3]. China is also funds for the development of the Hambantota port and Colombo Port City in Sri Lanka, Gwadar port in Pakistan etc. Aids are also given in terms of financial assistance like long-maturity bonds, low interest loans etc to these countries to ensure their support and participation in the project.

South Asian Region and Its Geopolitical Importance

Soon after the discovery of sea routes to India by Vasco Da' Gama and his arrival at Kozhikode port in 1492, there was a sudden inflow of sailors and merchants from the European continent to the South Asian region in search of new settlements and for precious goods like pepper, cotton, indigo, opium etc. Though the initial purpose of the arrival was purely of

China's One Belt One Road connectivity

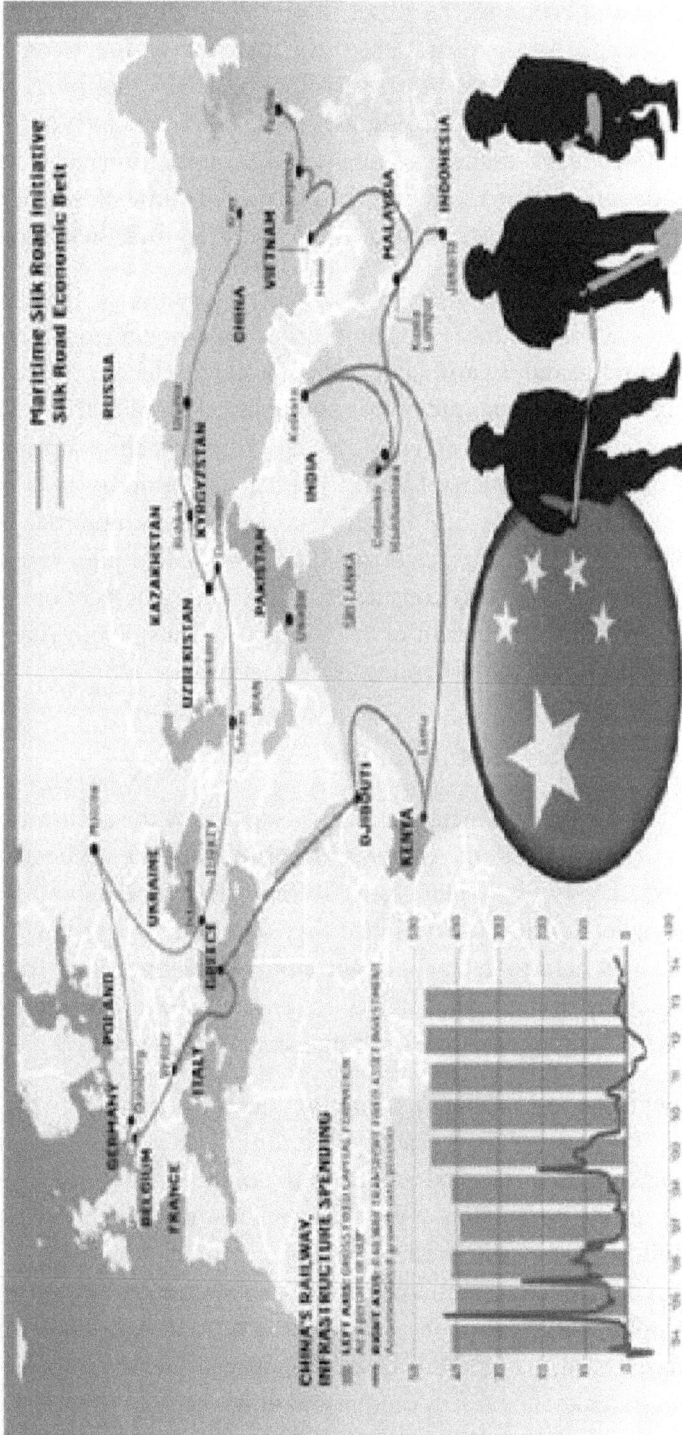

Source: www.independent.ie

commercial and economic purposes, soon they started to conquer these regions in South Asia and brought them under their direct control and administration. It was only in early 1940's and 1950's that most of these colonized countries attained freedom. India in 1947, Maldives in 1965, Sri Lanka in 1948 are few examples. Long years of colonization had resulted in the degradation of their economies and during the time of independence from imperialistic powers, most of these countries and their economies where in a state of ruin.

However, these countries in South Asian region, being the storehouses of rich natural resources and larger stock of human labour force, started to grow in terms of economic power and political stability from the mid-1960s. Today, South Asia is emerging as one of the most important regions in the world. The fulcrum of world politics and economics is shifting towards Asian continent. The South Asia region has a nominal GDP of \$2.9 trillion[4] and is the largest exporter of goods like jute, rubber, tea, coffee, cotton etc. It is also considered as the emerging economic force, having an overall GDP growth of 8.3% in 2008[5]. Thus, South Asia would play a significant role in the coming 'Asian Century'.

South Asia and her cultural unity

Protected by the great Himalayas in the North and by the semi-arid desert regions in the West, South Asia was insulated from the influence of the cultures which grew and replenished elsewhere in Central Asia and Middle East. The region traditionally has had very significant contacts with outer world but was able to retain its own culture and tradition. Today, the cultural identity of the region shares common characteristics in terms of similarities in religion, cuisine, clothing patters, languages etc.

Though the region shared a common heritage and culture for a long period of time, changes took place within the last six decades. The process of emergence of new national identities in South Asia became faster and evident from the early 1950s, a period which saw several countries in the region quitting imperialistic administration and attaining independence. As they become sovereign and independent, these countries chose different paths of politics and methods of development. In several instances they purposefully tried to impose a different national identity and collective behaviour to make themselves unique and different from the rest.

South Asian Unity and Challenges for India

As mentioned before, there must be greater efforts to create a sense of unity and trust in the region in order to reap the benefits of global economic growth. A major challenge faced by South Asia today is how to unite and harmonize the common culture and heritage that the region shares without harming the national identities and individualities of the member states. As the region is intertwined in terms of geography, culture and economy, there must be mutual trust and faith between the South Asian nations to move forward in the path of progress.

Being the largest country in terms of geographical area, economic output, human resources etc. the role of facing the challenges of regional integration lies on the shoulders of India. In order to bring unity and trust, India must take the lead role. However, this process of reconciliation and unification is not an easy task. It must be remembered that most of the South Asian nations were colonies at one point of time. Thus, South Asia is going through a 'post-colonial syndrome', in which the smaller and weaker nations of South Asia blindly oppose South Asian regional integration and possibilities of free trade. In the opinion of E .Sridharan, "There exists an obsession with sovereignty, initially the result of the colonial experience, evolved on the part of neighbouring states into a defensive mode against the possible Indian domination. Even if New Delhi doesn't act threateningly, the mere possibility of its regional domination elicits a defensive response from its neighbours."[6]

India's neighbours, fearful of its formidably larger size and power, fear of its domination over the smaller ones in the region, are sceptical and suspicious of India and do not cooperate fully with it on its political and security concerns. India's policies towards her neighbours over the last few decades have proved terribly ineffective. Most of the foreign policies of India with regard to these countries are always self-centric and hard-nosed. Though our country was able to achieve a steady economic growth of 7% to 8 % per annum, most of the neighbouring countries fall below of India's economic growth. This growing disparity will always act as a challenge as well as a threat to India primarily because of two reasons; one, growing disparities in the region will lead to an arrogant and boorish behaviour from the part of these neighbouring countries. Lack of economic consensus and financial cooperation was always a reason behind the fall of alliances and covenants in history. Another challenge posed by the neighbouring states to India is the growing impact of the foreign powers in terms of political as well as economic influence. India's response towards its neighbours was always in such a way that its created a vacuum or a free space for the entry of other superpowers like U.S.A, China etc. who can turn their economic influence into political interests in these countries and thus questions the supremacy enjoyed by Delhi in the South Asian region.

Role of Sri Lanka in MSR

China considers Sri Lanka as one of the most important partners to be cooperated in the MSR project is primarily due to its geographically significant location in the Indian Ocean. Compared to several other South Asian countries who are invited to be a part of the MSR initiative, Sri Lanka possesses certain qualities which make it fit to be a game changer. First, it's geographical significance in the Indian Ocean. Sri Lanka has the potential to act as the intermediary hub in the silk route which extends from Fuzhou port in China to African coast of Mozambique. Since maritime navigation requires refuelling facilities in between, by developing ports in Sri Lanka, China can provide uninterrupted fuel and resource supply to the marine vessels which transit goods through the sea route. Second, Sri Lankan participation in this project is to persuade New Delhi, who is unwilling to join the MSR. Due to the close proximity of Sri Lanka to Indian peninsula, India can't afford a strong Chinese presence in the island nation with Delhi acting as a bystander.

Sri Lanka is one of the three major committed partners in the MSR in the Indian Ocean region, the others being Bangladesh and Maldives. Soon after unveiling the MSR project in Indonesia in late 2013, Xi Jingping became the first Chinese president to visit the island nation in the last three decades. Beijing believes that without the cooperation of Sri Lanka, the MSR project's initial phase stretching from Eastern Chinese ports to Bangladesh and Myanmar to Sri Lanka and then to the Eastern Africa will be impractical. Colombo's new port developed and funded by China, will act as a maritime connection between the Persian Gulf and East Asia. The proposed Colombo Port city along with Hambantota port will be the only port in South Asia in the Indian Ocean that can lodge 18-meter deep draft vessels and vessels meant for faster logistics transfer in the Maritime Silk Route.

Factors Responsible for Sri Lankan Interest in MSR

Economic Factors

If the proposed MSR project yields the expected results, it will create a state of bliss in the island nations' economy which was affected by natural calamities and civil war for a long period of time. After attaining independence from Britain in 1948, Sri Lankan economy primarily relied upon the agricultural sector which mainly produced commodities like tea, coffee, rubber, tobacco and coconut. Later economy shifted relying on primary sector to service sectors like tourism, software outsourcing etc. In spite of the average growth of the economy at a rate of 7 to 8 per cent per annum, Sri Lankan economy faced financial recession several times. In 2001, Sri Lanka faced bankruptcy, with foreign debt reaching at 101 per cent of GDP[7].

Today, China is one of the largest trading partners of Sri Lanka. It is also one of the biggest lenders to the Sri Lankan economy. In recent years, China provided more than $6 billion as grants and loans to Lankan economy. Chinese tourists form the 5th largest arrivals to the island nation whose tourism sector contributes 3.7% of its GDP[8]. Once the MSR project is effective, this will boost the economy of Sri Lanka. Due to its geographic location in Indian Ocean Region (IOR), Sri Lanka will become the important trade hub between the Eastern Chinese ports and Eastern Africa. Hence, by joining MSR, Colombo can reap a lot of economic benefits which will in turn curb the issues like growing inflation, higher unemployment rates and market failures.

Political and Social Factors

It is not only the economic factors that make MSR attractive to Colombo but also the political and social factors which prevail. As mentioned before, Sri Lankan populace was deprived of economic progress and wellbeing for a long period of time. Social and political factors also contributed to this poor state of Sri Lankan society and thus to the overall progress of the society. Sri Lanka went through a situation of fear and insecurity due to the malicious Tamil insurgency lead against the Sinhalese dominated government by the Liberation Tigers of Tamil Elam (LTTE). This ethnic conflict, which started around 1979 and lasted till late 2009, created instability in government machineries and decision making process. Though the relations between the Colombo and New Delhi where cordial in nature for a long period of time, Tamil insurgency always remained as a challenge. From the time of her independence, the ethnic conflict between Sinhala majority and Tamil minority posed a threat to the unity and integrity of the island nation. India was also very sensitive to this issue as there was always a 'Pro-Sri Lankan Tamil' sentiment in South India and often played a crucial role in regional and national politics. Often, India's policy makers faced a trade-off between respecting the regional Tamil sentiments along with keeping cordial relations with Sri Lanka. This trade-off often resulted in framing ineffective foreign policies towards Sri Lanka, which in turn made Colombo suspicious of India's ability to protect and support the island nation in terms of military assistance and financial aids. Tensions between Delhi and Colombo reached its heights when the Sri Lankan government granted permission to a US based radio station to function in the island in the 1980s. By granting permission to the Voice of America radio, India suspected that, Colombo was allowing other foreign powers like USA, Pakistan, China, etc to snoop India. This security concern became the core reason in Delhi's decision to send Indian Peace Keeping Force (IPKF) in 1987. However, this decision backfired and worsened the relations between the two neighbours. On the other hand, LTTE retaliated by the assassination of Rajiv Gandhi in 1991. Politically, India's hands got tied as neither it could support the Sri Lankan government to suppress the Tamil insurgency nor to bring the LTTE in the path of peace and cooperation. This diplomatic standoff with India made the field free for other foreign nations like Pakistan, China and USA to become more active and influential in Sri Lankan politics.

This trend continued till recently as India often abstained from voting or voted against Sri Lanka whenever a resolution came up in UN regarding the genocide crimes committed by Colombo while wiping out the LTTE from Lankan soil. Such defects in the Indian approach towards the island nation are the main reasons for the growing Chinese influence in the island nation. With the proposals of MSR, Sri Lanka finds China as a stable ally who can lend support to the island nation in terms of financial and military assistance. However, with the new dispensation under the Prime Minister Ranil Wickremesinghe, India Sri Lanka relationship is growing steadily.

MSR and India: Concerns, Dilemmas and Challenges

India was formally invited by China to join the MSR in February 2014. Invitation was made by China's Special Representative Yang Jiechi during the 17th rounds of border talks. Though India's initial response was positive, later she took the stand that any further decision will be made only after "building mutual trust, stability, respect, free flow of commerce and ideas"[9].

India is primarily concerned about the nature and purpose of the MSR initiative as China hasn't released any detailed blueprint of the proposal so far. Moreover, India is suspicious of the Chinese efforts to increase its influence in the region at a time when India enjoys economic and political dominance in the region. The growing tensions between Sino-Indian relations and China's attempts to put India at a disadvantaged position in the political and economic arenas must be also taken into consideration while understanding the issue.

Economic and Financial Implications

China boasts MSR as the most innovative idea, for the South Asian region, which can turn the upcoming 'Golden Decade' of the region into a 'Diamond Decade'[10]. The proposed project, which connects 14 least-developed, economically backward regions of the Chinese Mainland with more than 55 countries, will boost the Chinese economy, which is struggling to maintain steady real economic growth, after taking the inflation rates into consideration. Due to the 2008 subprime crisis, global economy is also going through a financial crisis. As a result, there is a steady decline in the FDI inflows and import orders from US and EU, who are the largest trading partners of China. Thus, through MSR initiative, China will gain a lot of economic benefits.

However, MSR possess a trade-off situation for India. First, if India is joining the MSR, it will result in a huge inflow of cheap Chinese goods to the domestic Indian market. Though this situation is favourable for the Indian consumers, it will badly affect the local sellers and producers. With the introduction of such goods, there will be a constant decline in the demand for the domestic goods. This will also result in higher trade deficit between India and China. Thus, opening the markets to the Chinese goods must done with great caution. Secondly, if Sri Lanka and other South Asian countries join MSR and Delhi decides to not take part in it, Indian economy will be left out from the progress and growth brought by the silk route. Also, in many sectors, India face stiff competition from the South Asian countries; in the case of Ayurveda and tourism from Sri Lanka, Fisheries from Maldives, Software outsourcing from Indonesia etc.

Third important concern regarding economy is that once the MSR starts functioning, it will lead to the Chinese dominance in the domestic markets of South Asian countries. This will reduce the volume of exports from India to those South Asian countries. For several decades, India was Sri Lanka's largest trading partner with total transactions worth $1.7 billion in 2013[11]. The same applies to several other South Asian nations. Thus, the growth of the Chinese economy through the MSR will be at the cost of Indian economy.

Political and Geostrategic Implications

MSR will help Beijing to improve her relationship with the participating countries as there will be a large inflow of Chinese funds to these countries in the form of financial aids and economic funding. The relationship of Beijing with her immediate neighbours like Japan, Philippines, and Thailand etc is not smooth and stable, primarily due to several border disputes and Chinese activities in South China Sea. Thus, it has become important for China to get out of the image of 'an arrogant, unstable nation' who puts its interests over the interests of others to a 'more stable, trustworthy, benevolent state' who can act as a support to the smaller nations of the region. With the help of MSR, China can achieve this motive easily. Another implication is that China wants to increase its presence in the Indian Ocean. By doing so, China can put India, who now enjoys hegemony in the region, at a disadvantaged position. Also, it is very important for China to ensure safety and security of the vessels which carry goods, especially those through the Strait of Malacca.

India has also concerns regarding the Chinese intentions behind the MSR. Delhi seriously doubts the credibility of Beijing's portrayal of MSR as an initiative purely meant for the economic progress of China as well as the South Asia. Delhi fears that MSR will not only have a single dimension of economics but also that of military and defence. Recently, the arrival of two Chinese submarines at Lankan ports raised security concerns in India.

Many experts on Sino-Indian relations think that MSR is the modified version of the String of Pearls strategy.

Preferential Policies for India in Maritime Silk Route Initiative

MSR brought India into a state of dilemma as there are numerous benefits as well as detriments. In an age of multilateralism and growing cooperation between India and other countries, it is not a good idea to oppose an initiative which will lead to greater regional integration and economic returns. On the other hand, it must not be a win-lose situation in which India might sacrifice her regional dominance and economic interests. Hence, Indian policy makers must devise the plan on MSR taking all the factors into consideration.

While participating in the MSR, India must be vigilant about any action from the part of Beijing which can put India at a disadvantaged position. There must be attempts to balance the power relations between Delhi and China so that we can maintain status quo in the region. India must also rejuvenate SAARC (South Asian Association for Regional Cooperation), an organization where India enjoys supremacy and influence, to coordinate and bring the South Asian nations like Sri Lanka and Maldives together. Such efforts for regional cooperation will help the region from further interventions or influence of foreign nations.

Though India signed a Free Trade Agreement (FTA) with Sri Lanka in 1998, to a certain magnitude this agreement was a failure as there were a lot of commodities in the negative list. If a commodity is categorized under a negative list, there won't be customs relaxation over that commodity. Being the larger nation, there must be an effort from the part of India to relax existing trade barriers and must ensure free economic flow to strengthen ties between two neighbours.

Another outcome of the research is to strengthen India's maritime presence culturally, strategically and psychologically through the implementation of 'Project Mausam'. The undertaking is seen as the Modi government's most significant foreign policy initiative intended to counter China and her MSR. However, the project must be fruitful and shouldn't lack teeth like several other foreign policy initiatives of the past. Through the project, India can bring cultural integration in the region. Another suggestion is to increase the interaction between human capitals. That is, there must be efforts to give students and young minds of the region to interact with each other by University collaborations, educational exchange programmes etc. Recently established South Asian University at Delhi is a good example for such initiatives. India is also planning to launch a SAARC satellite by the end of 2016 to meet the growing communication needs of South Asian nations[12]. India can ensure its influence in the region also by introducing an Emergency Economic Fund (EEF) to fund and finance the South Asian nations during the time of market failures and financial crisis. This will ensure economic stability in the region, which will in turn prevent the South Asian nations from associating themselves with foreign powers for financial aids. India must also endeavour to raise its sea ports and hubs into international standards so that the total volume of trade carried out by them annually will increase.

Conclusion

MSR initiative is undoubtedly the most innovative initiative of the century, which can lead to overall development of the region, if implemented properly. However India, being the most powerful of the region, must act cautiously in order to maintain the influence and authority that she enjoys in the region. Indian Ocean Region is often projected as the most inconsistent, unstable region of the world[13]. Hence, every future policy regarding the countries like Sri Lanka must be taken with great caution. And with keeping great vigilance and care, India can also reap economic benefits from the Maritime Silk Route project.

Endnotes

1   Pandya, A. A., Herbert-Burns, R., & Kobayashi, J. (2011). Developments in Key Indian Ocean Trades. In *Maritime commerce and security: The Indian Ocean* (pp. 44-48). Washington, DC: Henry L. Stimson Center.

2   Aneja, A. (2015, March 30). China unveils details of ambitious Silk Road plans - The Hindu. Retrieved from http://www.thehindu.com/news/international/china-unveils-details-of-ambitious-silk-road-plans/article7048921.ece

3   Sri Lankan Port Authority. (2014, October 15). Re-imagining the Silk Route. Retrieved August 20, 2015, from www.slpa.lk/news_events_14104.asp

4   World Bank. (2015, March). South Asian Data compiled under Global Economic and Financial Analysis. Retrieved on August 24, 2015, from http://data.worldbank.org/region/SAS

5   Asian Development Bank. (2009, April). ADB Annual Report 2008, available at http://www.adb.org/documents/adb-annual-report-2008

6   Sridharan, E. (2011). *International relations theory and South Asia: Security, political economy, domestic politics, identities, and images.* New Delhi: Oxford University Press, p. 68.

7   Winslow, D., &Woost, M. D. (2004). *Economy, culture, and civil war in Sri Lanka* (2nd Ed.). Bloomington, IN: Indiana University Press.

8   Ibid.

9   Press Information Bureau. (2014, September 16). Transcript of Prime Minister's Interaction with Chinese media organizations, available at http://pib.nic.in/newsite/mbErel.aspx?relid=109728

10 "Move to Enhance Trade with ASEAN Countries: China Plans Maritime Silk Road". *The Asian Age* October 7, 2014.

11 Sikdar, C., & Chakraborty, D. (2012). *Bilateral trade between India and Sri Lanka – does factor content matter?* International Input-Output Association, available at   http://www.iioa.org/conferences/20th/papers/files/792_20120430061_Bilateraltradebetweenindia-srilanka-chandrimasikdar&debeshchakraborty.pdf

12 "SAARC satellite launch likely in December 2016", *The Hindu* July 14, 2015

13 World Bank. (2007). *The World Bank annual report 2007,*Washington D.C., available at http://goo.gl/HJ71Sn

Chapter 10

China's Footprints in Maldives: Concern for India?

Surendra Kumar

The way the foreign policy of China has evolved in recent decades to consolidate its interests could be an object lesson to other countries. Initially, China's Asian policy focused on North-East and South-East Asia. But in recent times, South Asia has gained tremendous importance in China's foreign policy, which currently aims to maintain and promote regional peace and stability and, in consequence, sustain China's own peaceful rise. Also, as India began to look eastward, China began to look southward to counter India's rise. In this context, South Asia constitutes an important region for China's strategic ambit, and Maldives is no different.

China-Maldives Relations: The Factors

Maldives was not strategically vital for the colonial rulers. The archipelagic nation being poorly endowed with resources and an insalubrious climate, with its terrain being dotted with dangerous coral reefs. India was an exception in that, it commenced diplomatic ties with its South Asian neighbour quite early, and unlike China, India established its ties immediately after Maldives attained independence from British colonial rule in 1965. Thus, China ties with Maldives began late, however it has deepended in recent times.

Political and Military Ties

China's relations with Maldives began slowly, but intensified with China's quest for global power. Maldives in October 1972 established formal relations with China, when the Chinese ambassador to Sri Lanka was concurrently accredited to Maldives. The two countries' bilateral relations improved with high-level visits between the two countries, which began with the Maldives Foreign Minister Jamil's visit to China in 1980, followed by President Maumoon Gayoom's visit in 1984.[1] This trend intensified in the 1990s, as Maldives became vital for China's interest in providing safe passage to its merchant ships and accessing the sea lanes in the Indian Ocean.[2] Since then, the relations have improved further, with bilateral high-level visits. The Maldives Foreign Minister and Defence and National Security Minister have regularly visited China. This has been reciprocated by Chinese Foreign Minister, Vice-Chairperson of the Standing Committee of the National People's Congress, Chairman of the Central Committee, General Chief of Staff of the PLA and Premier respectively in 1980 and 1990s.

In 2002 the two countries celebrated the 30th anniversary of the establishment of their bilateral diplomatic relations, with President Jiang Zemin and Foreign Minister Tang Jiaxuan exchanging congratulatory messages with President Gayoom and Foreign Minister Jameel, respectively. In September 2002, at the invitation of China's Central Military Commission, the Maldives State Minister of Defence and National Security visited China, which was the first official contact between the Chinese and Maldives armies. President Gayoom's visit in September 2006 further deepened the relations between the two countries. Maldives opened its embassy in Beijing in May 2009, and Ahmed Latheef was appointed as Maldives' first Ambassador to China. Party delegations from Maldives also visited China, to further ensure diplomatic cohesion. The visit by President Xi Jinping to Maldives in September 2014, in his first visit to South Asia, in a way indicated the balance-of-power dimension with India. President Xi was accompanied by a 100-member business delegation, demonstrating the economic focus of the visit.

In 2012, China and Maldives celebrated the 40th anniversary of the establishment of their formal bilateral ties, with Wu Bangguo, the Chairman of China's Standing Committee of the National People's Congress of China visiting Maldives. This was the first of its kind by a top Chinese legislator to the island. Bangguo emphasized during his visit that the relationship could be developed as a model between big and small nations. He also expressed the desire to open a Chinese Embassy in Maldives and promised to increase China's aid to Maldives to US $15.4 million. Direct flights were announced to Maldives and scholarships were offered to Maldivian students in 2012 and 2013.[3] In September 2013, a government delegation from Maldives attended the International Day of Peace Activities in China and the China-South Asia Peace and Development Forum. Political ties were further deepened with China opening its Embassy in Maldives in January 2014. It may be noted that China is the only non-South Asian country to set up an Embassy in Maldives, in order to cater for the needs of the large number of Chinese tourists visiting the archipelagic nation.

A military aid agreement was signed between the two countries in 2012. Initially, China's interest was to set up a military base in Maldives. But this objective has now taken a back seat with Sri Lanka forthcoming in meeting some of China's key maritime interests and with China not interested in antagonising the US and India, who are other security partners of Maldives. Nevertheless, there are reports that Beijing is still wooing Male to pre-empt a US move to set up a new military base in Maldives' southernmost island of Gan.[4]

Trade, Investment and Aid

Economic and technological cooperation between China and Maldives has also been growing over the years since 1981. Direct trade between the two countries has been growing since 1982, reaching US $2.977 million in 2002, of which Maldives exports were worth just US $2000, the imports from China being mainly rice and consumer goods. Bilateral trade went up to US $64 million in 2010, a rise of 56 per cent from 2009. With China providing concessional loans and investments to Maldives particularly in the fisheries sector and aquatic products, bilateral trade increased to US $98 million in 2013 and US $104 in 2014.[5] In recent times, China is an emerging market for Maldives marine products like yellow-fin tuna and sea cucumber. Furthermore, the two countries have initiated a feasibility study on free trade agreement (FTA) in February 2015. According to the Maldives Minister for Fisheries and Agriculture, "The biggest advantage of the free trade will go towards fishermen. With the free trade, 12 per cent export duty will be gone, thus the 12 per cent becomes profit for fishermen".[6]

There are a number of reasons for the growing bilateral economic ties, like several bilateral agreements and Memorandums of Understanding (MOUs), such as the Agreements on Economic and Technical Cooperation, Mutual Exemption of Visas and Visa Fees, on Education Cooperation, on Cultural Cooperation and various other important areas of mutual interest. These agreements have increased the number of Maldivian people visiting China for trade and business, in a way making China a most preferred destination for Maldivian traders. Apart from this, Maldives' liberal trade regime, increase in the number of Chinese tourists to Maldives, and China offering its state owned companies preferential loans to enable them to contribute to infrastructure building in the island, have strengthened the bilateral economic ties. The preference for China for Maldives' economic growth was well articulated by President Abdulla Yameen in November 2014 in that "Western colonial powers' " economic cooperation with China does not challenge Maldives' Islamic identity.[7]

On the investment front, Beijing is actively involved in several renewable energy projects, tourism and telecommunication sectors in Maldives. The Chinese investment increased from 1985 onwards. By the end of 2001, the accumulated volume for Chinese companies contracted projects in Maldives reached $46.37 million, with their turnover reaching $40 million. The projects included a 1000 Housing Units Project in Hulhumale, the National Museum, housing for the Ministry of Culture and Heritage, roads, and drainage systems in Male.[8] Significant major Chinese investments in Maldives include the bridge project connecting the airport and the capital. This has helped the archipelagic nation's tourism by ensuring that 30 to 40 per cent of the tourists are Chinese. To attract more investment and trade from China, Maldives has set up an office in Kunming, China.[9]

Chinese investment in Maldives got a boost with Vice President Mohamed Jameel Ahmed visiting China in June 2014, followed by President Xi Jinping's visit. The two countries agreed to cooperate on developing Special Economic Zones (SEZ) and construction of harbours and bunkering facilities.[10] The contract to expand Male airport was given to the Beijing Urban Construction Group after the Maldivian government cancelled a $511 million deal with India's GMR Infrastructure two years earlier.[11] When India protested this development, the Maldivian government emphasized that the Chinese firm does not have the right to run the airport for security reasons. An agreement has also been signed for the Male-Hulhule bridge, connecting the capital with its international airport. President Xi Jinping said in Male that he hoped that the bridge would be named China-Maldives Friendship Bridge.[12]

In a significant move, on 22 July 2015, the Maldivian Parliament (Majlis) amended the constitution and approved by 70 votes (14 against) foreign ownership of land in the country, which many argue will be beneficial to China. Members of Parliament voting against the move said that allowing investment of more than $1 billion could be used by China for its military expansion in the Indian Ocean region and would be detrimental to Maldivian national security interests.[13] India also expressed its concern. But the Maldivian government argued that the bill was intended to strengthen Maldives' economic ties with China, rather than military ties. It may be noted, however, that if China's level of economic activity in Maldives increases exponentially, China may usurp India's advantage of being Maldives' third-largest trading partner.

Over the decades, Chinese aid and investment to Maldives have also deepened the economic ties. China's aid to Maldives in the 1970s was RMB74.7875 million. As noted earlier, Beijing, as a part of its aid programme, constructed a building to house the Maldives Ministry of Foreign Affairs, a National Museum, and is involved in the 1000 Housing Units Project. President Abdulla Yameen visited China in August 2014 and secured a $16 million grant aid from China, which is expected to cover the costs partly of the Malé-Hulhule Bridge and other projects. China also provided emergency aid in December 2014 when Male's sewage treatment plant suffered a fire, leaving some 100,000 people without access to safe drinking water. It sent nearly 700 tons of fresh water and a Chinese Navy submarine rescue ship named *Changxing*, which could produce over 70 tons of desalted water every day.[14] Hence trade, investment and aid over the years have transformed the bilateral ties, for the beneficial of both the countries.

Tourism

The tourism industry accounts for about 70 per cent of Maldives' GDP, both direct and indirect via transportation, communication, and construction sectors. Maldives attracts a million tourists annually, of which Chinese tourists numbered 35,000 in 2008-9, and it increased to 363,626 in 2014, which accounted for one-third of arrivals, with 30 per cent market share.[15] Boosting the Chinese arrivals are, besides the resplendent beauty of the archipelago, direct flights from Beijing, Shanghai, Guangzhou, Kunming, Chengdu, Chongqing and Hong Kong to Maldives.[16] Chinese companies are also involved in promoting tourism in Maldives like China Union Pay (CUP), which has begun cash withdrawal services for cardholders in 95 per cent of ATM in Maldives after entering into partnership with Maldives' biggest bank in March 2010.[17] Apart from this, a joint venture has been initiated between the two countries to expand tourism. For example, China's Guandong Beta Ocean and a Maldivian company were awarded Vaavu Atoll Kunaavashi to develop a five-star luxury resort with some 142 rooms.[18] The Maldivian Tourism Ministry in May 2014 also signed an MOU with the state-owned China Machinery Engineering Corporation (CMEC) to develop Thaa Atoll Kalhufahalafushi as a resort. The Tourism Ministry has also launched the Visit Maldives Year 2016 campaign in its efforts to boost tourism to the country.

Maritime Dimension

Initially, China's objective in Maldives was to establish a military base in the archipelagic nation. The objective has, however, evolved in course of time leading to the following Xi-Yameen joint statement in September 2014:

> "We have agreed to jointly build the 21st Century Maritime Silk Road and take this opportunity to enhance cooperation in the fields of maritime economy, maritime security, ocean research, environment protection, and disaster prevention. We will also try to start some key projects that can yield quick results, at an early date".[19]

By endorsing MSR, Maldives seeks to promote itself as a vital trade-cum-transit port. China is encouraging this ambition by mapping the MSR through the Ihavandhippolhu Integrated Development Project, or iHavan which is in the northernmost atoll of Maldives. Thus, in recent times, the maritime dimension has gained greater significance in bilateral ties.

Why this is happening?

India has had strong historical, cultural, political and socio-economic relations with Maldives. But in recent years Maldives has developed closer ties with China. Some of the reasons why Maldives prefers to deal with China are as follows:

(a) Most of the Chinese projects are completed on time, unlike projects undertaken by Indian companies, such as the construction of the Indira Gandhi Memorial Hospital, which took an inordinately long time to complete; also, the quality of its construction is regarded to be poor.[20] An important feature of India's aid diplomacy in South Asia is that while it is generous in extending largesse, project deadlines are rarely met. Also, the major part of India's aid goes towards building capacity and developing democratic institutions, whose outcome is difficult to evaluate. Apparently, land ownership in Maldives requires $1 billion, which China has an advantage that its investment policy is friendly and less bureaucratic. In India, it would be difficult to get consensus on investing such a huge amount. According to Prof. Mahendra P. Lama, a South Asia analyst, China's political system allows it to go ahead with huge investment without concerning itself about domestic considerations, while in India, there are "domestic constituencies and angles to look into before starting a project in a foreign land".[21] Also, according to Prof. Lama, India has only "conventional cultural, economic or diplomatic ties and has not been able to create and establish any strong Indian constituencies, and our policy towards Maldives has been heavily government-centric."

(b) Human rights, democracy and rule of law play a vital role in determining India's relations with other countries, which is not the case with China. For example, when recently the Government of India protested against the ill treatment meted out to the former President Nasheed by the present Yameen government, the Maldivian Foreign Minister, Dunya Maumoon, remarked his government "will not take instructions from a foreign government [India]".[22] Even earlier, the Indian government imposed travel restrictions and some economic sanctions in response to any move to destabilising democracy in the archipelagic nation. On the other hand, responding to the current political crisis in Maldives, the

Chinese Foreign Ministry spokesperson Hong Lei remarked that the issue "is the domestic matter of the Maldives. ... China upholds the principle of non-interference in other countries' domestic affairs. We believe the Maldivian side can deal with its domestic affairs properly."[23]

(c) From time to time, China has come up with big selling ideas, which are being positively endorsed by the neighbouring countries. For example, the Maldives government has backed the Chinese-initiated Asian Infrastructure Investment Bank (AIIB). It has also responded positively to China's proposal for an FTA, which is now being pursued. Maldives has also joined China's ambitious MSR project and its 'One Belt One Road' Initiative. Thus, these Chinese initiatives have deepened the ties

(d) On the occasion of the Maldives' 50th Independence Day (July 2015), Prime Minister Narendra Modi called Maldives a "valued partner" of India, but in reaction to the ill treatment meted out to former President Nasheed, he did not visit Maldives during his tour of Indian Ocean countries in August 2015. Even India's Foreign Secretary S. Jaishankar had to postpone his visit to Maldives during his SAARC Yatra for five months, indicating India's displeasure with Maldives' internal developments. Thus, all these aspects favour Maldives to engage with China, rather than with India.

India's Response

India, enjoys a strong historical, diplomatic and cultural ties with Maldives. However, bilateral ties have been challenged by China's footprint in Maldives. In this context, India's response has been to work on the strong historical foundations. New Delhi was among the first countries to establish diplomatic ties with Male. Although India always emphasizes on promoting democracy, it extended support to the authoritarian rule of Maldivian President Maumoon Gayoom for thirty years. India even sent its naval contingent to stymie an attempt to overthrow the Gayoom government by some Sri Lanka-based dissidents in 1988. Over the decades, New Delhi has been Male's Big Brother, the most influential foreign power in Maldives (and also in Bhutan). India-Maldives relations were so significant that

Maldives even sought to purchase land in India for relocating its citizens in case they become environmental refugees as a result of climate change and rising sea levels. However, in recent times, Australia and the US have emerged as alternative options to Maldives.

The bilateral ties have also been a result of strong naval interaction between the two countries. According to the Indian Ministry of Defence (MOD), Maldives has more interaction with the Indian Navy and Coast Guard than any other country in the Indian Ocean.[24] Over the decades, India has also helped Maldives set up its coastal surveillance capabilities. Recently, India was the first country to respond when Male's sewage treatment plant damaged, leaving many people without access to safe drinking water.

India is a major economic partner of Maldives. However, the relationship has faced hurdles after Maldives cancelled its contract with GMR (an Indian company) and gave the contract to a Chinese company for major investment in Male airport. The Indian government nevertheless continues to provide development aid and cooperation to Maldives without any conditionality to promote South-South cooperation, building solidarity and partnership between developing nations and good-neighbourhood policy. Generally, in the 1980s and 1990s India's aid to the archipelagic nation went towards building its long-term educational and health infrastructure. However, Indian aid intensified in 2007 in response to China's mounting interest in Maldives.[25] In a significant move, the Indian government has hiked its aid allocation to Maldives from $4 million in 2014 to $30 million in 2015-16, indicating the enhanced priority it accords to Maldives.[26] Although Maldives' share in India's total aid is just 2 per cent in 2015-16, its share has undergone a roughly sevenfold increase from last year.

Both India and China are striving for maritime dominance in the Indian Ocean Region (IOR). China has been consolidating its commercial maritime interest in the region, while India has given importance to maintaining security.[27] In July 2013 India signed a tripartite maritime security agreement with Sri Lanka and Maldives, to address common maritime security threats, challenges and also to enhance security primarily through cooperative measures. These involve joint cooperation on exclusive economic zone (EEZ) surveillance, search and rescue (SAR) operations, working on anti-piracy efforts, sharing and tracking of merchant vessels using new technology.[28] All these would be addressed through Maritime Domain Awareness (MDA), Long Range Identification and Tracking (LRIT), Merchant Ship Information System (MSIS) and Automatic Identification system (AIS), SAR coordination including training, develop marine oil pollution response, and exchange of information on illegal maritime activities through channels of communication.[29]

This agreement also caters to the needs of Maldives. Although sea areas between India and Maldives are not chokepoints, they are very wide and can be termed high seas strategic passage way, where the bulk of merchant traffic funnels in and out. The huge amount of traffic might result in accidents, pollution affecting the marine environment, and tourism and fishing industry, on which Maldives direly depends.[30] Moreover, the Somali sea piracy has come close to the shores of Maldives and India. There have been a number of incidents of capturing Somali pirates in Maldives waters, exposing the vulnerability of this archipelagic nation. This aspect is addressed in the agreement. There is also the factor of terrorism launched from the sea. Overall, India's policy towards Maldives is guided by its good-neighbourhood policy and protecting its interest in IOR. This was well articulated by India's then Prime Minister Manmohan Singh in November 2011. When addressing the Maldivian Parliament he said, "This is our extended neighbourhood, we wish to work with the Maldives and other likeminded countries to ensure peace and prosperity in the IOR".[31]

Possibility of 'Chindia' (China+India) in Maldives

Although in recent times both India and China are asserting their interest in Maldives, there are many areas where they can cooperate in their own interest and also in the interest of Maldives. For instance:

(a) India can assist Maldives and other littoral states in their quest for economic growth and it can also offer to train their human resources and transfer technology. China in its turn can enhance its aid for infrastructure development. This will ensure that Maldives and other Indian Ocean nations will progress while maintaining good relations with both China and India. Both countries should realise that competition will only lead to the small states fearing both military hegemony and economic monopoly, which affects the growth of the region.

(b) Economic and energy security are prime strategic interests for India and China. The two countries are among the largest economies in the world and are keen to secure markets for exports, obtain raw materials, energy resources and enhance their international stature. Their economic resurgence is directly linked to their overseas trade and energy needs, most of which are transported by sea. India's imports and exports have reached $500 billion already and may well touch $2 trillion by 2020.[32] Also, India depends for 70 per cent of its fossil fuel on imports, whose figure is estimated to rise to 85 per cent by 2020. Many Indian security analysts believe that energy security will be India's prime strategic interest for the next 25 years. China also depends on overseas resources and energy supplies, especially oil and natural gas from the Persian Gulf and Africa. It is forecast that China's oil consumption would increase by 150 per cent by 2020 and its foreign supplies will be more than 75 per cent.[33] In addition, both India and China want the protection of Sea Lanes of Communication (SLOCs), prevention of economic degradation and climate changes in the region. In this regard, Maldives becomes important as it sits along major sea lanes, including the East-West shipping route through which much of the Middle East oil headed for East Asia is transported. The archipelago is located just 340 km from the Indian coast.

(c) Maldives told the United Nations in 1987 that a 2.01168 metre rise in sea level could submerge the whole country, and since then it has been highlighting the issue of climate change at all global forums. Both India and China are supporting the Maldives campaign on climate change. For example, when the US rejected the Kyoto Pact (1997) on global warming, China termed it as an "irresponsible decision". Both India and China have interacted with Maldives at successive international climate change negotiations, particularly at the Copenhagen summit, 2009. Both India and China can use new technology and support Maldives' cause at the global and regional levels.

(d) Maldives faces the potential of rising Islamic extremism. For instance, in 2010 some Maldivians were arrested in Pakistan for terrorist activity and training at camps in South Waziristan.[34] This extremism could be a threat to Maldives and the region, affecting the interests of both India and China. There is also the possibility of terrorist groups trying to recruit members in Maldives, which will certainly affect its tourism and economy. Both India and China fear that especially in the context of rising religious radicalism in Maldives, anti-India terror groups will take root there and seek sanctuary in the many uninhabited islands of the archipelago. These anxieties have prompted India and China to intensify cooperation with successive Maldivian governments.

As regards balancing India and China in the context of Maldives, then President Nasheed said in May 2011: "I don't think we have to walk a tightrope. We are firstly a SAARC member country and China's friendship is about broader global interest rather than regional."[35] In the interest of Maldives and the region, both India and China should work on a win-win situation through cooperation, rather than confrontation and competition, which will affect Maldives' growth and prosperity.

Endnotes

1   Kumar, Anand (2012)."Chinese Engagement with the Maldives: Impact on Security Environment in the Indian Ocean Region", *Strategic Analysis*, 36(2), p. 283.

2   Karambelkar, Amruta (2011)."Wu Bangguo's Visit to the Maldives", *View Point* (ICWA), 22 June, p. 2

3   Ibid.,

4   "GMR-Maldives spat: China behind scrapped GMR deal to extend footprint in Maldives?" *The Economic Times*. 15 December 2012.   Available at http://economictimes.indiatimes.com/articleshow/17622309.cms?utm_source=contentofinterest&utm_medium=text&utm_campaign=cppst

5   "China and Maldives"(2015). Available at www.fmprc.gov.cn/mfa_eng/wjb_663304/zzjg_663340/ yzs_663350/gjlb_663354/2737_663478/ and see "China, Maldives launch feasibility study on FTA", *Xinhua*, 2 June 2015. Available at   http://www.chinadaily.com.cn/business/2015-02/06/content_19507615.html

6   Humaam Hamid, Ismail (2014). "Maldives backs new Chinese investment bank, pursues free trade deal", December 22. Available at http://minivannewsarchive. com/politics/maldives-backs-new-chinese-investment-bank-pursues-free-trade-deal-91768#sthash.Xb69wx5Q.dpuf

7   Masood, Asma (2015). "India- Maldives- China: Strategic Relations" C3S Paper No. 0003, 7th July   Available at http://www.c3sindia.org/uncategorized/4753

8   Kumar, Anand, op.cit. 1, p.281

9   Op.cit.5.

10 Kondapalli, Srikant (2014), "Maritime Silk Road: Increasing Chinese Inroads into the Maldives", Institute of Peace and Conflcit Studies, No. 4735. Available at www.ipcs.org/article/china/maritime-silk-road-increasing-chinese-inroads-into-the-maldives-4735.html

11 Bosley, Daniel (2014). "Maldives gives airport contract to Chinese firm during Xi's visit", Available at http://in.reuters.com/article/2014/09/15/china-maldives-idINKBN0HA1TS20140915

12 Masood, Asma, India- Maldives- China.

13 Sharma, Rajeev (2015). "Maldives tweaks law on foreign freeholds, China likely to edge India on investment", 24 July. Available at http://www.firstpost. com/world/maldives-tweaks-law-on-foreign-freeholds-china-likely-to-edge-india-on-investment-2362070.html

14 "Chinese Government Continues to Provide Emergency Assistance to the Maldives", 8 December 2014. Available at http://www.fmprc.gov.cn/mfa_eng/ wjb_663304/zzjg_663340/yzs_663350/gjlb_663354/2737_663478/2739_66348 2/t1217941.shtml

15 Variyar, Mugdha (2015), "Chinese 'Land Grab' in Maldives: How India Can Counter Beijing's Expanding Sphere of Influence", 27 July. Available at http://www.ibtimes.co.in/maldives-land-ownership-why-india-should-be-concerned-what-should-it-do-counter-china-640594 and see "Maldives' tourism industry faces challenges as Chinese tourists decline", Xinhua, 2 February 2015. Available at http://www.chinadaily.com.cn/travel/2015-02/26/ content_19660540.htm

16 Op.cit.5.

17 Raman, B.(2010)."China in Maldives", C3S Paper, No.458, 7 March. Available at http://www.c3sindia.org/maldives/1237

18 Hamid, Ismail Humaan, (2015). "Chinese investment in Maldives tourism 'expected to rise", 11 June. Available at http://minivannewsarchive.com/politics/chinese-investment-in-maldives-tourism-expected-to-rise-99406#sthash.fcW6XbhC.dpuf

19 Kondapalli, op.cit.10.

20 Kumar, Ananad, op.cit. 1, p.281

21 Variyar, Mugdha, op.cit. 15.

22 Panda, Ankit (2015), "India's Maldivian Headache", 26 February. Available at http://thediplomat.com/2015/02/indias-maldivian-headache/

23 Ibid.,

24 Samaranayake, Nilanthi (2012). "Maldives; why the US and India should remain calm" *PacNet*, No. 13, 1 March, p.1

25 Ramachandran, Sudha, (2015), "India's surging aid to Maldives points to its strategic location ", *Asia Times*, 20 April . Available at http://atimes.com/2015/04/indias-surging-aid-to-maldives-points-to-its-strategic-location/

26 Ibid.,

27 Kahangama, Iranga, (2014),"India, Sri Lanka and Maldives: Tripartite Maritime Security Agreement and growing Chinese influence", in Bhattacherjee, Aparupa (eds.), "The Maritime Great Game: Indian, China and US and the Indian Ocean, " *IPCS special focus*, p.12

28 Ibid.,

29 Sakhuja, Vijay (2014), "India, Sri Lanka and Maldives: A Maritime troika leads the way" in Bhattacherjee, Aparupa, op.cit.27,p.14.

30 Ibid.,

31 Samaranayake, Nilanthi, op.cit.24, p.1

32 Das, Premvir (2011), "Maritime Power: Key to Indian Security Interest, *Policy Paper Series*, No.1, January,p.9.

33 James R. Holmes, Andrew C Winner and Toshi Yoshihara, (2010), *Indian Naval Strategy in the Twenty-first Century*, Longon: Routledge, p.129

34 Samaranayake, Nilanthi, op.cit.24, p.1.

35 Karambelkar, Amruta, op.cit.2, p. 3.

Chapter 11

Sub-regional Cooperation: Diversities and Linkages

V. Suryanarayan

In this contemporary world, no country, however powerful, can chart its destiny alone. It has been the lesson of history that governments can optimize their opportunities and enhance their capacity to shape events if they join a group of countries with shared political and economic interests. Despite the advantages of geographical contiguity and common historical and cultural heritage, the contemporary South Asian scene presents a picture of a house divided. The inter-state relations in South Asia, since the advent of independence, have been characterized by mutual suspicions, unfriendly relations and, at times, even open conflict.

The primacy of political and strategic consensus in viable regional organizations has been highlighted by several strategic specialists. Late K. Subramaniam, India's foremost strategic thinker, pointed out a few years ago that in those parts of the world, where regional organizations have taken roots, "it is based primarily on political and security consensus". In a similar vein, working out a balance sheet of regional co-operation in different parts of the world, Prof. Mohammad Ayoob remarked that there is a growing identity of approach and convergence of interests in four critical areas, where the idea of regional organization has succeeded, and those are: 1) Similarity of threat perceptions, both internal and external, which leads not only to identity of threat perceptions, but also to security co-operation in critical areas; 2) Identity of political systems which lead to common political ideological perceptions; 3) Common foreign policy stances on crucial global issues providing for a convergence of strategic perceptions and 4) An unwritten understanding of the role of pivotal power – India in the case of South Asia – which provides internal cohesion and lessening of inter-state tensions in the region.[1]

Many foreign policy commentators have praised ASEAN as a dynamic economic organization; however, it must be pointed out that its success had been mainly in the field of political co-operation, especially in the late 1970's. The formation of ASEAN itself was a political act, though political co-operation was not specifically mentioned in the ASEAN Declaration. On the 20th anniversary of ASEAN, Malaysian Prime Minister Dr. Mahathir pointed out, "In its first twenty years the main thrust of ASEAN has been political. This is, as it should be, and we have no need for regrets". Mahathir added "none of the ASEAN countries would have developed economically, if this political wrangling could not be solved". Ghazalie Shafie, former Malaysian Foreign Minister, elaborated this point further: " I can understand the frustration of those well meaning observers who would like to credit ASEAN with economic success, when there is precious little to talk about… ASEAN was the result of political declaration … And although ASEAN officials had repeatedly asserted in public that political issues were never discussed, in reality Ministers were able to wholly or partially settle many outstanding political issues among themselves that might have remained unresolved had they been aired publicly. Since the formation of ASEAN, there have been no contradictions that could cause serious concern".[2] Explaining the concept of "togetherness", which brought cohesion and unity to ASEAN, and more specifically the pivotal role of Indonesia, Ghazalie Shafie added: "ASEAN was likened to a cluster of bamboos, each of which was an independent entity, and which together could withstand turbulent winds; the tallest of the bamboos must always stoop its head. Indonesia is a large country, but it has never imposed its will on the other ASEAN members. In fact, when the Secretary General of ASEAN accompanied by a delegation of very senior ASEAN officials, visited the United States a few weeks ago, to explain the concept of EAEC, the spokesman was an ASEAN official from Brunei, the youngest, the newest and the smallest member of ASEAN". Adam Malik, the former Foreign Minister of Indonesia, echoed the same feelings. To quote Malik "Although from the outset, ASEAN was conceived as an organization for economic, social and cultural co-operation, and although considerations in these fields were no doubt central, it was the fact that there was a convergence in political outlook...which provided the main stimulus to join together in ASEAN".

While ASEAN during the third Indo-China War provided a shining example of regional co-operation, the South Asian Association of Regional Co-operation (SAARC) has yet to emerge as a united organization. During the eighth SAARC Summit, the Pakistani President, Farooq Ahmad Khan Leghari, pointed out that SAARC "has not taken off". Unlike the cluster of bamboos swinging in unison, the political elite of South Asia have become prisoners of their past and victims of domestic compulsions. They act as a drag against each other and are unable to articulate a common point of view in international forums. As Prof. Nancy Jetly has pointed out, "The need for initiating a new and more relaxed chapter in South Asian political relations ... is self-evident. There is no gainsaying the fact that a durable framework of co-operation in the region would have to be supportive of bilateral relationships. The hub of such co-operation would essentially rest on India's equation with its neighbours. As the largest and stablest economic power in the region, India has a special responsibility for setting the tone of bilateral relationships. Equally important, the smaller countries of the region cannot eschew the responsibility of building a climate of trust and friendship in the region. In the final analysis, India and Pakistan – constituting the fulcrum of South Asia – would have to develop the will and the capacity to resolve their long standing differences in order to build lasting bridges of trust and friendship".

Can India be bogged down by Pakistani Intransigence?

Can we allow Indian diplomacy to be bogged down by India-Pakistan differences? The only option for New Delhi is to build up the defence preparedness against Pakistan while, at the same time, persuading Pakistani leadership to give up its policy of supporting acts of terrorism against India. Simultaneously New Delhi should strengthen bilateral relations with other neighbouring countries on the basis of "asymmetrical reciprocity". India should take the initiative to form new forms of sub-regional organizations so that South Asia does not lag behind other parts of the world.

The concept of Ocean as a unifying force and as a focus of regional organisation has not yet been fully grasped. The Author, along with Prof. KR Singh, former Professor of Jawaharlal Nehru University, has been advocating the formation of a Bay of Bengal Community. When we use the term Bay of Bengal we also include the two adjuncts of Bay of Bengal, the Andaman Sea and the Malacca Straits. Historically the littoral states – India, Bangladesh, Myanmar, Thailand, Malaysia, Singapore, Indonesia and Sri Lanka – have witnessed dynamic interaction between maritime trade and cultural evolution. The Bay of Bengal is a gift of Mother Nature and co-operation among littoral states and can lead to a win-win situation for all. Moreover, unlike the South China Sea, which has become turbulent because of conflicting territorial claims and China's insensitive policy towards its maritime neighbors, the Bay of Bengal region is relatively calm and tranquil. Exploitation of maritime resources, promotion of tourism, weather forecasting and prevention of maritime terrorism – take any subject, fruitful co-operation can benefit all littoral states. The BIMSTEC (Bangladesh, India, Myanmar, Sri Lanka Technical Co-operation) came into existence in June 1997. It was renamed Bay of Bengal Initiative for Multi-Sectoral Technical and Economic Co-operation and was expanded to include landlocked states of Nepal and Bhutan. It has identified certain areas of co-operation, but the overall progress had been very slow. What is more, no attempts are being made to include the littoral states of Andaman Sea and Malacca Straits. Such an initiative is immediately called for to bring Malaysia, Singapore and Indonesia into the organization.

On this note, we should also acknowledge another sub-regional organization BCIM – Bangladesh, China, India, Myanmar sub-regional co-operation – which had been hitting newspaper headlines during recent years. The proposed regional co-operation will bring the Yunnan province of China closer together with northeastern India, Bangladesh and Myanmar. The inaugural BCIM meeting was held in Kunming in August 1999. Since then a number of meetings have been held, but here again the progress had been taking place at a snail's pace. The greatest obstacle to the progress of BCIM is China's territorial claims on Northeast India and the political instability in Northeast India, Myanmar and Bangladesh. Unless India-China territorial claims are settled and peace and stability returns to northeast India, Myanmar and Bangladesh the full potentials of regional co-operation cannot be accomplished. What is more, a closer study of the neighborhood policy of India and China would reveal that both Beijing and New Delhi are laying greater emphasis on promoting bilateral co-operation than giving a fillip to sub-regional co-operation. The BCIM is also closely linked to developing Northeast India as a gateway to Southeast

Asia. India has a lot of connection with neighboring states of Bangladesh and Myanmar and if these connections are exploited to the full it will lead to all round progress. It should also be highlighted that the Chinese goods are flooding the markets in northeast India through illegal trade. China gets all the benefit though this illegal trade without any corresponding benefit to India.

India, Sri Lanka, Maldives sub-regional co-operation

The sub-regional co-operation consisting of the island Republic of Sri Lanka and the archipelagic state of the Republic of Maldives as well as the southern part of South India (Tamil Nadu and Kerala), is an innovative idea and deserves serious consideration by the policy makers in New Delhi, Colombo and Male. The three units have the potential in terms of natural and human resources to co-operate with one another in transforming Southern part of South Asia into a vibrant and prosperous region.

Diversities and Linkages

In this section I have attempted to highlight the diversities and linkages within and among the three member countries. *The People of India,* a research project of the Anthropological Survey of India, attempts to provide the cultural profile of all communities in India, the impact of change, and linkages and diversities among them. An interesting conclusion deserves special mention. Communities, cutting across religion, share a great many cultural traits. Thus the Hindus share a very high percentage of traits with Muslims- 97.7 per cent; Buddhists -91.9 per cent; Sikhs- 88.99 per cent, and Jains - 77.46 per cent. Other communities that share a high percentage of common cultural traits are Muslims- Sikhs 89.95 per cent; Muslims-Buddhists – 91.28 per cent and Jain-Buddhists – 81.34 per cent. As KS Singh, former Director-General of the Anthropological Survey of India, has remarked: "Diversities and Linkages, freedom and tolerance go together". [3]

As a result of cultural interaction among various communities the Indian culture has emerged as a composite culture. All religions, philosophical traditions, cuisines, art and architecture, language and music have provided cultural efflorescence to the region. The influence of the Hindus and the Muslims on one another can be seen in music, architecture, dress and food. The *sufi* movement of Islam and the *Bhakti* movement of Hinduism represented the blending of religions in India.

Few illustrations of the composite culture in the realm of religion in Tamil Nadu and Kerala need special mention. When I was associated with the Calicut University, Kerala a few years ago as the first Professor for Maritime Studies I came across an interesting variant of Ramayana popular among the local Muslims called the *Moplah Ramayana.* The Muslims in Malabar followed the *Marumakkathayam* (matrilineal) system, till such time the Mohammadan law was enacted by the legislative assembly of Madras Presidency. Thousands of Hindu pilgrims from all parts of the world throng the Ayyappa temple in Sabarimalai, but before they reach Sabarimalai, they offer worship in a Muslim *Dargah* known as *Vavar Kavu.* The Maulavi applies *Vibhuti* (sacred ash) on their foreheads. Bava (vavar) is considered to be the brother of Lord Ayyappa, the presiding deity of Sabarimalai. The most melodious Hindu religious songs in Malayalam, Tamil, Kannada and Telugu are sung by a Christian, Yesudas. The land for the construction of the tank near the Kapaleeshwar temple in Mylapore was donated by the Nawab of Arcot. One of the greatest authorities in Kamba Ramayana was a Muslim, Justice Ismail. According to tradition, Lord Vishnu in Sri Rangam is reported to have married a Muslim woman *Tulukka Nachiar* and the first offering to the Lord everyday is *Roti.* The Masjid in Nagore and the church in Velankanni are holy places visited by Christians, Muslims and Hindus.

The greatest illustration of India's composite culture was Mohammad Abdul Kalam, former President of India, who passed away recently. A devout Muslim, he grew up in an eclectic environment in Rameshwaram and embodied in himself the noblest qualities of Indian culture. A Muslim steeped in Hindu traditions, a scientist who could recite verses from *Thirukkural,* an artist who played the Saraswathi Veena, a scholar who was well versed in Quran, Geetha and the Bible, and, above all, a great teacher he is a role model for all Indians.[4]

South India-Sri Lanka linkages

India, especially South India, has left abiding cultural influences in Sri Lanka. All aspects of Sri Lankan life – language, culture, religion, literature, art and architecture – bear the indelible imprint of Indian cultural forms.

In the course of his visit to Ceylon in 1927, to popularize Khadi and prohibition, Gandhiji rightly referred to Ceylon as India's "daughter state".[5] But the asymmetrical power equation made the Sinhalese deeply suspicious of India's aims and objectives. Later, when the ethnic conflict began, tendentious writers both among the Sinhalese and the Tamils started to project the two communities at war with one another for several centuries. It reminds one of the famous statements of French political philosopher Voltaire, "If you believe in absurdities you will commit atrocities".

Historians and archaeologists specializing in South Asian history are of the view that the sea separating Sri Lanka and South India is a unifier and the lands on either side of it were parts of a single cultural group. In his fascinating book, *The evolution of an Ethnic Identity,* Prof. K. Indrapala has pointed out that South India should not be treated as an alien country when we study the early history of the island[6]. In the pre-historic and proto-historic periods, Prof. Indrapala argues, the southernmost parts of India, mainly the modern Indian states of Kerala, Tamil Nadu, parts of Karnataka and Andhra Pradesh formed a single cultural region with the Palk Strait/ Gulf of Mannar as a unifier. He adds that even after the emergence of two states, there was a two-flow of influences, particularly in art, religion and technology. This point of view is also shared by other well known historians like Prof. Sudarsen Senivaratne, Prof. Leslie Gunawardena and Prof. Paranavitana. In fact, the evolution of two ethnic identities, Sinhalese and the Tamil took place at a later stage in the beginning of 13th century.

Prof KS Singh has pointed out that in India there are several communities that can be classified as having more than one religion. It is interesting to note that Sinhalese religious practices also point to the same direction. The Hindu Bhakti cult has influenced Theravada Buddhism and there are images of Hindu Gods in Buddhist temples. The deity of *Skanda* (Muruga) in Kataragama, situated near the Yala sanctuary in the southeast of the island, continues to be the major "institutional intersection of several religious faiths … all go to Kataragama, where the atmosphere is one of tolerance and goodwill".[7] During my last visit to the temple few years ago I found Buddhist pilgrims outnumbering the Hindus. The Sinhalese carry the *Kavadi* with great devotion and fervor. Few Sri Lankan scholars want to subscribe to the objective truth that Buddhism was a virile religion in South India and the spread and efflorescence of Theravada Buddhism in the island has much to do with fruitful contacts with Buddhist centres of learning in Kancheepuram, Kaveripatinam and Madurai. Buddhaghosha of Magadha, "poet, philosopher and commentator" of Theravada Buddhism, was patronized by Sanghapala, the King of Kancheepuram.[8] It is a matter of pride for the Tamils that one of the greatest epics of Theravada form of Buddhism is in Tamil language. *Manimekhalai,* written in the 2nd century AD, is one of the finest jewels of Tamil Buddhist literature.

Kerala's relations with Sri Lanka and interaction with the Sinhalese and the Tamils remain a neglected area of historical research. According to Prof. Gananath Obeysekere, when Hinduism began to dominate the religious scene in Kerala from tenth century, large number of Buddhists migrated to Ceylon and they got easily assimilated with the Sinhalese population. There are surnames like *Kuruppu,* the name of a Hindu Nair sub-caste in Kerala, among the Sinhalese population. The spread of the cult of Goddess *Pattini* in the island is an illustration of benign interaction among various religious groups. It is also a pointer to the ingratiating and assimilable qualities of the peoples of South Asia.

The distorted vision of India and Tamil Nadu in Sinhalese minds has been aptly summed up Late Prof. Urmila Phadnis as follows: "While Sri Lanka continues to look upon North India as the cradle of its religion, it perceives its contacts with South India, particularly with Tamil Nadu, as having been by their very nature a source of perennial concern for its integrity as a nation state".[9] To look upon dynastic rivalries for territorial expansion as an expression of enmity between India and Sri Lanka or between the Sinhalese and the Tamils or between the Buddhists and Hindus will lead to falsification of history. Prof. Anuradha Senevaratna, Professor of Sinhala in Peradeniya University, in his book, *The Lions and the Tigers: Religious and Cultural Background of the Sinhala-Tamil Relations,* provides certain interesting facts: "In the war between Elara and Dutugemunu, there had been Sinhala commanders fighting for Elara, while the Sinhala king Dutugemunu had commanders of South Indian origin".[10] In times of political unrest in the island, the Kings of South India "would have found it politically expedient to invade the country". Sometimes, as part of political strategy, the Sinhala kings took the assistance of South Indian kings to strengthen their position against their rivals. Prof. Senevaratna adds: "whenever there was trouble in Sri Lanka, whether it was political unrest or famine, the Buddhist monks made a habit of escaping to South India for safety. South Indian Dravidian monks also followed the same example. Sri Lankan kings made grants available to Tamil monks".[11]

Looking at the past through the prism of the present

To look at the past through the prism of the present can lead to falsification of history. The projection of Sinhalese and Tamils as two antagonistic entities, at war with each other for several centuries by Sinhalese/Tamil chauvinist writers, two sides of the same coin, is an illustration of the well known axiom that truth and objectivity are the first casualties in times of conflict. Eric Hobsbawm has pointed out, "history is the raw material for nationalist or ethnic or fundamentalist ideologies, as poppies are the raw material for heroin addiction". Stanley Tambiah, after years of painstaking research, has come to the conclusion that Sinhalese and Tamils share many parallel features of "traditional caste, kinship, popular religious cult, customs and so on. But they have come to be divided by their mythic characters and tendentious historical misunderstandings of the past".[12] He has also exploded the myth of racial divide which states that the Sinhalese are fair Aryans and the Tamils are dark Dravidians. Quoting Gananath Obeysekere, Tambiah adds, "Biologically speaking, those we call Sinhala are in fact racially inter-mixed with South Indian peoples and with aboriginal groups like the Vedda; and the Tamils who live in the north and the east are also similarly biologically mixed".

It is my contention that the roots of the ethnic conflict have to be traced to the post independence period, especially after 1956, when the Sinhalese leaders wanted to build the nation on the basis of the language and religion of the majority people, ignoring the legitimate demands of minority groups- Si Lankan Tamils, hill country Tamils and the Tamil speaking Muslims. What is more, in times of conflict, realities get relegated to the background and perception becomes important. And the perception among the Sinhalese majority, a majority community with a minority complex, is that the Sri Lankan Tamils are determined to carve out a separate state for themselves through violent means.

Tamil Nadu factor

The competitive nature of Tamil Nadu politics, with the two Dravidian parties, Dravida Munnetra Kazhagam (DMK) and the All India Dravida

Munnetra Kazhagam (AIADMK), competing with one another as to who is the saviour of the Tamils overseas casts its long shadow over India-Sri Lanka relations. In that process, political gimmicks become more important than positive contributions to ethnic reconciliation. The unanimous resolution passed by the Tamil Nadu Legislative Assembly that former President Mahinda Rajapaksa should be tried by the International Court for genocide committed during the last stages of the Fourth Eelam War will in no way help in bringing about peace and stability in the island. There are immense benefits if the shipping service between Rameshwaram and Talaimannar is resumed, but the Tamil Nadu Government has not evinced any interest in the subject. Similarly the proposal to construct a land bridge between Rameshwaram and Talaimannar is also cold shouldered by the AIADMK government. On the fishermen issue Chief Minister Jayalalitha turns a Nelson's eye to the reality that the problem has arisen as a result of indiscriminate bottom trawling by the Tamil Nadu fishermen in Sri Lankan waters. Tamil Nadu universities can attract large number of Sri Lankan students; but they hesitate to come to Tamil Nadu because they are not sure whether they are welcome. Few years ago the overzealous Tamil fanatics attacked a bus which was carrying Sri Lankan pilgrims to Velankanni, incidentally most of the pilgrims were Tamil Christians. In terms of concrete steps for the rehabilitation and reconstruction of the war affected Tamil areas in Sri Lanka, the contribution of Tamil Nadu had been minimal.

Maldives – Rejection of Diversity

The democracy in Sri Lanka has led to many acts of discrimination against the minority groups as a result of which the Tamils find it difficult to protect, foster and promote their cultural identity. The Islamic Republic of Maldives is still worse; it does not want to give any political space to the minorities at all. According to the Constitution of Maldives only Sunni Muslims can be citizens. Others can be residents and continue with their employment, but they do not have religious or cultural rights. Unlike other plural societies there are no churches, temples or chaityas. When a visitor arrives in Male airport he is not expected to carry the religious texts – Bible or Bhagvat Geetha- nor the portraits of Hindu Gods or Christian saints. Maldives has a rich cultural heritage dating back to the glorious days of Mesopotamian civilization, but the Maldivian government completely ignores pre-Islamic Hindu-Buddhist heritage. The archaeological relics relating to this glorious period in Maldivian history are kept in gunny bags and kept outside the main building in the museum, exposed to the ravages of the sun and the rain. The Islamic clergy do not encourage excavations which may provide details of the pre-Islamic period. In fact a perusal of history text books reveals that the official history of Maldives starts only with Islamisation of the archipelago. The legal system is based on *Sharia*.

The long spell of authoritarianism under Abdul Gayoom was brought to an end by a democratic upsurge led Mahammad Nasheed who was also elected as President of Maldives. But the reactionary forces ganged up against him and forced him to resign. The new government has framed trumped charges against him for treason and has detained him. The international community including India is pressurizing the Maldivian government on release Nasheed, but the government remains adamant.

How should India respond to the unfolding situation in Maldives? India responded spontaneously when the Maldivian government faced an attempted coup in 1988, which enabled Gayoom to remain in power. The Indian armed forces are also deeply involved in patrolling the outer limits of the maritime territory. New Delhi is interested in having friendly governments, committed to democracy in neighbouring countries and naturally its sympathies are with Nasheed. In fact Prime Minister Narendra Modi called off his visit to Maldives at the last moment which was a signal that New Delhi was unhappy with the anti-democratic acts of the present government. In her recent visit to Male, the Minister for External Affairs Smt Sushma Swaraj has reiterated India's commitment to the restoration of democracy. In a world of shrinking geographical boundaries and widening intellectual horizon no country, least of all Maldives, can afford to go against democratic tide. moreover, India cannot afford to follow a foreign policy of cynicism and opportunism as China does - supporting the genocidal Pol Pot- Ieng Sari clique in Kampuchea, arming and bankrolling the nuclear programmes of Pakistan, providing legitimacy to the military junta in Myanmar and supporting the genocidal policy of Mahinda Rajapaksa in Sri Lanka.

Conclusion

I would like to conclude the essay with a quotation from TS Eliot's *Four Quartets*. To quote: "What we call the beginning is often the end. And to make an end is to make a beginning. The end is where we start from". In the introductory part of the essay, I pointed out that in those parts of the world where regional organizations have succeeded there had been a convergence of political interests and, what is more, political systems which subscribe to the same ideals. The objectives of the sub-regional organization consisting of South India, Sri Lanka and Maldives are laudable. But unless ethnic reconciliation takes place in Sri Lanka and democracy is restored in Maldives, the prospects for sub-regional co-operation look very bleak.

Endnotes

1   Mohammed Ayoob, "The Primacy of the Political: South Asian Regional Cooperation (SARC) in Comparative Perspective", *Asian Survey* , Vol. 25, No. 4, pp. 443-457.

2   Jorn Dosh, "Southeast Asia and the Asia Pacific: ASEAN", in Michael K. Connors, Rémy Davison, Jörn Dosch, *The New Global Politics of the Asia Pacific*, New York: Routledge, 2004, p. 51.

3   Lertrit, Patcharee, "Mitochondrial DNA history of Sri Lankan ethnic people: their relations within the island and with the Indian subcontinental populations," *Journal of Human Genetics*, Vol. 59, 2014, pp. 28–36.

4   A K. Ananthanathan, *Temple, Religion and Society, East and West*, Vol 43, No. 4, 1993, pp. 155-168.

5   Tyronne Fernando, Alien *Winds across Paradise: A New Look at Sri Lanka's Foreign Relations through the Ages*, Vikas Publishing House, 2002.

6   K. Indrapala, *Evolution of An Ethnic Identity - The Tamils in Sri Lanka : C 300 BCE to 1200 CE,*

7   Ibid

8   Keerthi Jayasekera, "Arhant Mahinda in South India and Sri Lanka," *Daily News*, 2 June 2004 at http://archives.dailynews.lk/2004/06/02/fea61.html

9   Patrick Peebles, *The History of Sri Lanka*, Greenwood Publishing Group, 2006.

10 Silva, K.M. D', *A History of Sri Lanka*, New Delhi: Oxford University Press, 1981

11 "Sacred Kapilavastu Relics arriving in Sri Lanka", available at http://www.mea.gov.lk/index.php/en/media/news-archive/3563-sacred-kapilavastu-relics-arriving-in-sri-lanka

12 Tambiah, Stanley J., *Sri Lanka: Ethnic Fratricide and the Dismantling of Democracy*, University Of Chicago Press, Chicago, 1991.

Chapter 12

Sub-regional Maritime Security Challenges: A Cooperative Approach

Udai Rao

The Indian Ocean has today emerged as the centre of gravity of the world in the maritime domain. The eminent US Naval strategist Captain Alfred Thayyar Mahan had said as far back as 1890 that "Whoever controls the Indian Ocean will dominate Asia. This ocean is the key to the Seven Seas. In the 21 st century the destiny of the world will be decided in its waters". A very prophetic statement indeed. India's centrality in the Indian Ocean needs no emphasis. The Indian Peninsula juts into the North Indian Ocean like a springboard, dividing it into two almost equal halves. The Indian Ocean has the Asian land mass as a rooftop and is land locked from three sides with access largely from the Southern approaches and through the choke points of Hormuz, Suez Canal, Gulf of Aden, Straits of Malacca, Sunda straits and Lombok straits. Through these choke points pass the East-West Sea Lanes of Communications (SLOCs) which are the economic lifelines of the world, passing close to our shores and putting us in a very vantage position.

The Indian Ocean thus links the Atlantic and the Pacific Oceans. What is more important is that 66% of the world's oil, 50 %of the world's container traffic and 33% of the world's general cargo passes through the Indian Ocean. A significant point is that 80% of the world's trade which transits the Indian Ocean is extra –regional in nature. This means that any disruption in the free flow of trade through the Indian Ocean, can have a catastrophic impact on the global economy. More importantly over 90% of our trade by volume [1] including crude oil passes through the same SLOCs, so vital for our economic and energy security. To that extent India, washed as she is by three oceans, is actually an island country.

India shares maritime boundaries with seven countries, namely Pakistan, Bangladesh, Myanmar, Thailand, Indonesia, Sri Lanka and the Maldives; the last two being true island countries. In recent times the term 'Small Island Developing States' (SIDS)[2] is increasingly being heard on the world stage. Sri Lanka and Maldives belong to that category. Therefore if one were to talk of a sub –grouping under SAARC, India and the two island states of Sri Lanka and Maldives are perfect candidates for the sub-regional maritime grouping as we have much in common. Sri Lanka is our closest maritime neighbour, connected by an umbilical cord, the Ram Sethu, but separated by the Palk Bay, both physically and metaphorically due to the fishermen's problem. The Maldives which consist of about 1200 islands is about 400 NM from India and despite historically good relations; some irritations have crept into our relationship of late.

The tyranny of geography fortunately does not affect island states as it does the land states. The seas offer great connectivity facilitated by the principle of 'Mare Liberum' or the 'Freedom of the Seas', unlike on land. Therefore while land states may look at grouping based on contiguous neighbourhood, island states are not so bound. The seas have a transnational nature about them, permitting distant countries with even a modicum of sea faring skills to be neighbours.

By extension the question that arises next is why should the grouping be restricted to only countries under SAARC? The other prominent Indian Ocean island states of Seychelles and Mauritius may not be a part of SAARC, but the maritime medium makes them our neighbours and we need to transcend the South Asian sphere to connect across the global commons. After all India, Sri Lanka, Maldives, Seychelles and Mauritius have a lot in common in terms of history, culture, ethnicity, religion, commerce, Diaspora etc. These four island countries straddle the SLOCs in the Indian Ocean and also geo strategically dominate the approaches to the North Arabian Sea as also India. Unfortunately due to our continental mindset and perpetual obsession with Pakistan, we have neglected these maritime neighbours for far too long, much to our own detriment. Consequently extra regional powers like China have warmed up to them for their own strategic interests.

In its quest to be a regional power India has always considered itself as a 'Net Security Provider'[3] in the Indian Ocean Region (IOR) as highlighted by former Prime Minister Manmohan Singh a few years ago. Mr Narendra Modi soon after taking over as Prime Minster of India articulated the 'Act East Policy' which is our very own pivot. India now sees the Indo – Pacific as an integrated entity. PM Modi realises that his development agenda on the basis of which he came to power, 'Make in India' campaign, 49% FDI move and Blue Economy are all dependant on the safe seas. All most all of Modi's out visits therefore have had a strong maritime element with the obvious aim of shaping our maritime domain and the outcome documents are also replete with references to maritime security, maritime cooperation and china's intransigence in the South China Sea. Modi's visit to the Indian Ocean island countries of Seychelles, Mauritius and Sri Lanka earlier this year has to be seen in this light. Maldives unfortunately had to be excluded due to the treatment meted out to the former Maldivian president Nasheed.

Economy and Security are two sides of the same coin. Maritime security is like an insurance policy for national development. Therefore we need to build our own 'String of Pearls' to shape the security construct of our neighbourhood for mutual benefit. This can minimise the footprint of an extra regional power like China and make the area a secure and developing neighbourhood, where we resolve issues peacefully through dialogue, making India a fulcrum of stability.

India, Sri Lanka and Maldives launched the 'Trilateral Cooperation in Maritime Security' in October 2011 at the first NSA-level Trilateral Meeting on Maritime Security Cooperation in Maldives.[4] Seychelles and Mauritius are all set to include in the talk as they currently have observer status. This is indicative of the fact that the grouping with Sri Lanka and Maldives would be incomplete without Seychelles and Mauritius because of the common challenges we face at sea. The former NSA Shivshankar Menon had called the five countries the 'Indian Ocean 5'[5.] Nevertheless due to the scope that has been set out for the author, this article will deal largely with the trio of India, Sri Lanka and Maldives with brief references to Seychelles and Mauritius where pertinent.

When nation states decide to form a grouping or sub-grouping, they naturally would have to consider the environment including threats, challenges, opportunities, interests etc. The Indian Ocean which has an area of 68.5 million sq km, is home to many of these as elaborated below.

Threats at Sea

The biggest threat to maritime security in the Indian Ocean today is not from any conventional war, but from unconventional or asymmetric threats. Maritime terrorism tops the list, with piracy especially off Somalia, coming next. Smuggling, poaching, drug trafficking, illegal migration, movement of suspicious vessels, cargo and crew; people smuggling, gun running and narco-terrorism are all serious security threats too, since the machinery and network used for them could also be used for maritime terrorism as in the 1993 Mumbai blasts.

Maritime terrorism

We live in a troubled neighbourhood. Pakistan's state sponsored terrorism is well known to need any recounting here. In the last few years Pakistan has been channelling some of its nefarious activities to India through neighbourhood. A Pakistani diplomat based in Sri Lanka was reportedly involved in trying to ferment problems in the Southern States of India in 2014 as reported by the media[6]. Maldives has in recent years become increasingly radicalised with the active support of Pakistan. The problem of Islamic State of ISIS it appears is here for a long haul and could well singe us .Only last year the Al Qaeda leader Ayman Al Zawahiri had threatened to raise the flag of jihad in the Indian subcontinent, targeting India, Myanmar and Bangladesh[7]. Again in 2014 Taliban fighters had stormed the Karachi naval base and even tried to hijack a naval vessel 'Zulfiqar' to attack US Naval ships, something which could be attempted against us too[8]. All this is happening even as the US prepares to leave Afghanistan and is rebalancing to the Pacific which would create a vacuum to the North West of our country, with consequences for India. It is a well established fact that Al Qaeda, Taliban, Lashkar –e –Taiba (LET) etc have all got sea going skills [9]and could team up with other like minded organizations to carry out dastardly attacks at / from the sea.

As far as maritime terrorism is concerned we have indeed learnt the hard way. The 1993 Mumbai blasts for which arms and ammunition came across the seas may be a distant memory, but the 26/11 Mumbai attacks was definitely a more traumatic and humiliating experience- a 'Maritime kargil' so to speak. More recently we have had the Pakistani boat incident which blew itself up off Porbandar on 31 Dec 2014[10] and few months ago an Iranian boat[11]with Pakistani crew was apprehended off Kerala under suspicious circumstances.

Piracy

Piracy off Somalia which started in 2008   is thankfully on the wane after peaking in 2011 largely due to the efforts of multinational navies and embarkation of armed guards on merchant ships. Several Indians have been held hostage by the pirates, causing anguish to them and their families back home. The Indian Navy has constantly had a ship on patrol off Somalia since 2008 and has rescued mariners of several nationalities; not just Indians[12]. Pirates have operated over a large swath of the ocean, striking as far as off Seychelles and Mauritius and even India's Lakshadweep & Minicoy Islands. The menace of piracy has had a negative impact on the security, fishing and tourism industries of these island countries.

The Dragon in the Indian Ocean

But the biggest long term threat in the Indian Ocean is China. If anything has rekindled our interest in 'matters maritime', it is the surge of the PLA Navy into the Indian Ocean in the last decade or so. China's interest in the Indian Ocean stems largely from her desire for super power status and the fact that she is today the world's second largest economy. To fuel this economy, China imports 60% of her crude oil requirements from West Asia and West Africa through the choke points of Gulf of Aden, Hormuz, Malacca Straits, Cape of Good Hope etc[13]. India due to her geo –strategic position dominates these SLOCs and could interdict it in the event of a stand off with China. China, therefore, has been shaping the environment by assisting countries along the West Asia - Malacca axis.

String of pearls strategy

At the outset China has built ports and infra structure at Gwadar in Pakistan, Hambantota in Sri Lanka and Kyaukpyu in Myanmar in what has come to be known as 'String of Pearls Strategy'[14]. The rail, road and overland pipe network being built from Gadara to Kasha in Xinjiang province of China and the overland pipeline from Kyaukpyu in Myanmar to Kunming in Yunnan province would enable China to pump oil from West Asia directly to its hinterland thus avoiding the long logistic tail via the Indian Ocean and the vulnerable Malacca straits. She would also be able to use these channels to export finished products. Her presence in Hambantota and Colombo is akin to a Southern border being opened up for India. With footholds in the Arabian Sea (Gwadar), Bay of Bengal (kyaukpyu) and Hambantota, China automatically becomes an Indian Ocean power. PM Modi's visit to Vietnam and Japan and efforts to cement relations with them are obviously meant to return china's favour in her own backyard.

Anti-Piracy Task Force

It was, however, the advent of piracy off Somalia in 2008 that was the laboratory for China's surge in to the Indian Ocean. China first sent its three ships Anti Piracy Task Force[15] to patrol off Somalia in 2008 and today the 19th Task Force is on station. This has been an excellent training ground for an emerging Blue Water PLA Navy. The ships stayed for several months at a time in the area, with the accompanying tanker providing logistics. The ships have also called at various ports in the region such as Seychelles, Aden, Oman, Djibouti, Saudi Arabia etc for logistics. The Chinese have also used this opportunity to hold joint exercises and other aspects of maritime diplomacy with regional navies. Seychelles in fact had in 2012 reportedly offered basing facilities to China to support operations in the area[16]. China of course has denied any such plans. China thus has developed a legitimate and permanent naval presence in the IOR.

Submarine intrusions into the Indian Ocean

Simultaneously the US Navy had reported Chinese submarine intrusions into the Indian Ocean and later the Indian Navy too started reporting forays by Chinese submarines into the IOR. But it was the well publicised visits of a conventional submarine and later a nuclear submarine to Colombo in 2014 and more recently a Yuan class submarine's visit to Karachi that has sent alarm bells ringing in Delhi [17]which sees it as a subtle message from China of its growing maritime prowess.

New maritime silk route

But the Chinese masterstroke came in 2014 with the announcement of a $ 40 billion new Maritime Silk Route (NMSR) which envisages the building of ports, marine infrastructure, SEZ etc from China all the way to Europe along the seashore. Although projected as an economic initiative, it has underlying military and strategic objectives with serious implications for India. Sri Lanka, Maldives, Seychelles, Mauritius and several other countries have all signed up for NMSR[18]. These countries lack resources and therefore have opted to do what is best for them. India's coffers may not be overflowing currently, but it can still hold its own with some smart moves and need not compete with China.

India's Ministry of External Affairs (MEA) last year announced Project Mausam[19], presumably as an answer to China's NMSR, which is a throwback to our monsoon driven seafaring traditions. The details are very sketchy and how it will translate to present day maritime economics is not very clear. The MEA needs to explain this to our people and our neighbours so that the project can indeed take off.

Blue Economy

In the last few years the concept of a Blue Economy[20] has emerged largely from Small Island Developing States (SIDS) who find that the seas are more relevant to them than the 'Green Economy' being talked about by larger countries. This is the sustainable development of living and non living resources from the seas in an integrated manner and includes fishing, harbours, shipping & cargo; oil & gas exploration, ship building, sea bed mining, marine technology, marine tourism etc.

Maldives

Our geography and our alacrity have always ensured that we have always been first responders whenever Maldives has faced a crisis. In 1988 the Indian Navy led by INS Godavari successfully averted a coup in Maldives in an operation code named 'Operation Cactus'[21]. In 2004 after the Tsunami, the Indian Navy was quick on the scene to help Maldives, Sri Lanka and several other countries[22]. China surprisingly was conspicuous by its absence. This year when Maldives faced a drinking water crisis[23], the Indian Air Force (IAF) and our Navy swung into action, although China too did fetch up, albeit a little later.

The increasing radicalization of Maldives, President Yameen's pro-China tilt, the GMR fiasco, the arrest of former president Nasheed etc are not in our favour. China's investment in up gradation of Maldives International Airport, building of a bridge between Male and Hulhule, housing projects etc are worrying Delhi[24]. Recently Maldives has passed laws allowing foreigners to buy land provided they invest $ 1 billion and reclaim 70% of the land from the sea[25]. China has the money and the expertise to reclaim land, so this largesse is perhaps mostly intended for China and needs careful watching. Maldives incidentally has the largest no of tourists from China at 400,000 per year which indicates their warming ties[26].

Sri Lanka

Turning to Sri Lanka, the Tamil Nadu (TN) factor and its objections to training of Sri Lankan military personnel in India and India's principled stand on the UN resolutions on Sri Lanka's war crimes have all indirectly helped China and Pakistan, who have obviously capitalized on it. While we complain of China's investment in Hambantota the fact is that it was first offered to India and we kept sitting on it and did not do much to involve our private companies[27]. Similarly the control of Trincomalee was first offered to New Delhi in early 2000 but TN and LTTE were possibly the inhibiting factors[28]. Sri Lanka is bound to have a soft corner for China considering that in the final stages of its war against LTTE it was China that came to Sri Lanka's rescue, when India was handicapped in providing frontline equipment due to the TN factor.

After Maithripala Sirisena took over as President of Sri Lanka in 2015 and after PM Modi's recent visit to Colombo the relationship has regained some leverage. India has agreed to help make Trincomalee with its 99 Second World War oil storage tanks, a petroleum hub[29]. There is talk of India removing wrecks from Kankesanturai harbour in Northern Jaffna and making it navigable once again. Ferry services between Colombo and Tuticorin in Tamil Nadu could also be started.

As regards the Palk Bay and Katchativu, there are many number of views. The Centre has however told the Supreme Court that Katchativu was never ceded to Sri Lanka[30] and by implication there is no going back on Katchativu. Our side of the International Maritime Boundary Line (IMBL) has been overfished due to the bottom trawling method of fishing adopted by TN fishermen .On the other hand, the Sri Lankans have adopted better fishing practices and the suspension of fishing in restricted areas during the Eeelam war has helped the fish population multiply. Legally and diplomatically our fishermen cannot cross the IMBL into Sri Lanka. The only way out is to encourage   them to shift from traditional fishing to deep sea fishing. In the interim we need to look at fish farming in the Palk bay and Gulf of Mannar. Licensed fishing in Sri Lankan waters with the latter's approval   could also be explored. Till then the fishing wars have the potential to create diplomatic issues every few months and would be the biggest fishbone in our relations.

But it must also be said that Sri Lankan deep sea fishing vessels have also been intercepted fishing in India's EEZ both off the West and East coasts, though we do not go about shooting them, unlike Sri Lanka does[31]. Further, Sri Lanka has permitted Chinese trawlers to carry out licensed fishing in its EEZ, which has implications for India[32]. Also over 30% of India's cargo is transhipped at Colombo at the Chinese owned container terminals which pose serious security concerns[33]. Sri Lanka also needs to monitor the numerous Private Maritime Security Companies (PMSC) with their floating weapon armouries which have sprung up after the advent of piracy off Somalia and operate from Colombo [34].

Building Bridges across the Oceans

In the last few years the term 'Maritime Cooperation' has become a buzzword   during discussions between leaders and in   the outcome documents of their visits, as also in bilateral and multilateral fora. This is on account of the increasing importance of the seas. Cooperation at sea becomes necessary due to the sheer size and expanse of the maritime domain, due to which no nation has the resources to go it alone. The maritime domain offers great connectivity as mentioned earlier and there are no fences at sea unlike on land. The freedom of the seas allows us to cooperate keeping sovereignty issues in mind, i.e., without crossing the 12 NM territorial waters limit, if so required. The coming together of multinational navies to fight piracy off Somalia is a prime example of maritime cooperation.

There is tremendous scope for maritime cooperation between India, Sri Lanka, Maldives, Seychelles & Mauritius as elaborated below. The island states are still developing nations and require all the help they can get from India. They will try and play India and China against each other for their individual benefit and will have differences of opinion as well. But their sensibilities need to be respected. We however need to be alert so that anything which affects our national interest, especially where China and Pakistan are concerned is suitably addressed. Indeed, New Delhi should not force countries to choose between India and China. India's benign nature is there for all to see and China is perhaps its own biggest enemy. New Delhi needs to high light the peaceful resolution of the Indo- Bangladesh IMBL problem through the International Tribunal on the Law of the Sea (ITLOS)[35] in 2014 even though we lost a little more EEZ than what we had expected. In contrast China's disputes and aggressive stance in the South China Sea speaks for itself. A common complaint that is often heard is that India is slow in implementing projects, which is unfortunately is true. India needs to act on our promises quickly like China.

Maritime Domain Awareness (MDA)

A pre-requisite for dominating the oceans is Maritime Domain Awareness (MDA)[36]or situational awareness at sea. This has become critical after 9/11 and 26/11. The idea being to map all activities at sea so that one can decide what is normal and /or abnormal and thereby tackle illegal or suspicious activities. This can be done by a plethora of platforms and sensors such as ships and aircraft, Satellites, Unmanned Aerial Vehicles (UAVs), Long Range Information and Tracking (LRIT) which is satellite based, Automatic Identification Systems (AIS) which is V/UHF enabled, Coastal Surveillance Radars, intelligence inputs etc which are fused together to present a coherent picture to make the seas translucent.

During PM Modi's recent visit to Seychelles he commissioned a network of coastal radars. Seychelles will ultimately have eight radars, Mauritius eight, Maldives ten and Sri Lanka six radars[37]. This network of radars would share sensor data with participating countries and would be linked with Indian Joint Operations Centres (JOCs) at Mumbai, Vishakhapatnam, Kochi and Port Blair and the National Command, Control, Communication and Intelligence facility (NC^{3}I) at Delhi, thus enhancing our maritime domain awareness .

India has also entered into an agreement with 24 countries to share white shipping information on merchant ships[38], their cargo and crew.

The idea is to nab rogue ships carrying suspicious cargo or crew to ports of participating nations including in Seychelles, Mauritius, Maldives and Sri Lanka before they can strike. Merchant ship information obtained from Long Range Information and Tracking (LRIT) and Automatic Identification System (AIS) would also be shared. The 'Trilateral Maritime Security Cooperation Initiative' with Sri Lanka and Maldives and which is expected to include Seychelles and Mauritius soon, will also contribute to enhancing our MDA.

Humanitarian assistance and disaster relief (HADR)

It appears that navies are made for providing humanitarian assistance and disaster relief. The Indian navy's response after the 2004 Tsunami was indeed exemplary. This quick response earned India and its Navy worldwide kudos. More recently the Indian Navy carried out searches for the missing Malaysian aircraft MH 370 in the waters of the Andaman Sea and Bay of Bengal[39]. India's quick response during the drinking water crisis in Maldives early 2015 has been well appreciated. Further during the recent crisis in Yemen when people had to be evacuated[40]; the Indian Navy, a few of our merchant ships and the Air Force all swung in to action, rescuing not just Indians, but people of several nationalities.

Port visits / Joint exercises

Ships of the Indian Navy routinely visit the four island countries, making port visits and conducting joint exercises to inspire confidence and build inter-operability to tackle crises whenever they occur. The Indian coast guard conducts joint exercises with the Coast Guards of Sri Lanka and Maldives called 'DOSTI' which includes Search and Rescue (SAR), marine oil spill response, medical evacuation etc. Similarly the Indian Navy carries out joint exercises with the Sri Lankan Navy called 'SLINEX'[41].

EEZ patrol

Countries like Maldives, Seychelles and Mauritius have large Exclusive Economic Zones (EEZs) of 1.2 million sq km, 1.3 million sq km &1.27 million sq km respectively. However, they lack the resources to keep such large EEZs under surveillance against threats outlined earlier. Indian ships and aircraft often carry out EEZ patrol in the EEZs of Seychelles, Mauritius and Maldives[42] at their invitation which due to the transnational nature of the seas adds to our security.

Hydrographic assistance

India with its own hydrographic organization has been helping Maldives Seychelles, Mauritius etc map their oceans for safe navigation and exploitation of sea resources. The United Nations Conference on the Laws of the Seas (UNCLOS) and the impending expansion of the EEZ from 200 NM to 350 NM depending on the extension of the continental shelf underwater, has been a catalyst and has seen nations hurrying to map their oceans. During Modi's visit to Seychelles an agreement was signed for cooperation in hydrographic surveys and joint development of navigation charts[43].

Ocean science technology

India leads the region with many institutes on ocean science which could help the island nations. The Ministry of Earth Sciences (MoES) has a number of organizations such as the Centre for Marine Living Resources and Ecology, Kochi; Centre for Integrated Coastal and Marine Area Management, Chennai; National Centre for Ocean Technology, Chennai; and National Centre for Antarctic and Ocean Research, Goa which could help the island states address issues such as sustainable fishing, climatology, oceanography, meteorology, global warming, natural disasters etc.

Cooperation in Blue Economy

India with its huge scientific manpower pool and large scientific & industrial base is well suited to cooperate with the four island countries in oil & gas exploration, sea bed mining (India is a pioneer investor in Southern Indian ocean), ship building, ocean engineering, building of maritime infrastructure etc and in turn could benefit in deep sea fishing and marine tourism from them. India needs more civilian maritime projects and need to provide not just patrol ships but civilian ships of about 1000 tons with amphibious capability for better inter-island connectivity of these nations. New Delhi also need to encourage private companies like Larsen & Toubro (L& T) etc to compete for maritime projects in these countries like China Harbour Engineering Company (CHEC) and other Chinese companies.

It is interesting to note that while India is building medium sized Offshore Support Vessels (OPVs) for Sri Lanka[44], the latter in turn is building small interceptor craft for the Sagar Prahari Bal of the Indian Navy[45].

Capacity building

As far as capacity building is concerned, it is mostly about hardware, equipment and infra structure. During PM Modi's recent Indian Ocean visit he handed over a new Indian built patrol vessel to Mauritius called 'Barracuda' and promised a second Dornier aircraft to Seychelles. Earlier in 2014 a patrol vessel called 'Constant' and Indian built Dhruv helicopters were handed over to Maldives. The PM has spoken about building infrastructure on Assumption island in Seychelles and Agalega island in Mauritius[46] which could be a strategic asset for us especially in presence missions and in enhancing our MDA.

Training

For the last several decades India has trained a large number of naval officers and sailors from countries all over the globe in ab-initio courses as also advanced courses. The training is of a very high quality and at a fraction of the cost of that offered by Western countries. This has seen many countries including Seychelles, Mauritius, Maldives and Sri Lanka opt for Indian training. In fact Sri Lanka is the beneficiary of the largest number of training slots from India in recent times. The navy has undertaken diving and special forces training and training for Visit, Board, Search and Seizure (VBSS) operations for some of the island countries lately .

Maritime Multilateralism

India is a member of the 20 nation multilateral organization 'Indian Ocean Rim Association' (IORA)[47] based in Mauritius which deals with economic, cultural and political issues and indeed must also address maritime issues more effectively. Sri Lanka, Seychelles and Mauritius are also members of the IORA (China is a dialogue partner). There is however a need for India and other nations to infuse fresh energy into IORA to achieve comprehensive maritime security and economic development in the Indian Ocean. The Indian Navy launched the Indian Ocean Naval Symposium (IONS)[48] in 2008 as a construct to enhance maritime cooperation among the 35 member navies in the Indian Ocean Region. The aim was to promote shared understanding of maritime issues facing littoral nations and formulate strategies to enhance regional maritime security. India is also a founding member of the UN sponsored 'Contact Group on Piracy off the Coast of Somalia' (CGPCS)[49] and has made useful contribution in tackling piracy issues. The four island countries are also members of the CGPCS mechanism. The region also has a multilateral naval construct called 'MILAN'. It is a biennial event to enhance regional cooperation and is conducted at Port Blair. The last was held in Feb 2014 where 17 countries participated including the four island states. The Indian Navy will host its second International Fleet Review(IFR) [50]from 04-08 Feb 2016 at Vishakhapatnam to promote maritime cooperation and friendship. The slogan of the IFR is 'United Through Oceans' and will showcase ships from over 60 nations ,including the four island nations. With India, Sri Lanka, Maldives, Mauritius and Seychelles being members of several multilateral maritime organizations , there is much we can do together for security and cooperation at sea.

The Way Ahead

It is very clear that we need to build maritime bridges with our island neighbours to better engage them. We have been slow due to our lack of a maritime vision. Maritime issues including maritime cooperation can be handled better with a strong Maritime Governance structure at Delhi. In this respect the much overdue National Maritime Authority(NMA)[51] promised by the Modi Govt in June 2014 needs to be implemented as early as possible. This would bring about much needed coordination amongst the various maritime stake holders so that they act in complete synergy which would actually help PM Modi's 'Maritime Outreach' in big way. The NMA would help us script a more robust maritime vision and help us draw up a 'National Maritime Strategy for India' which hopefully would incorporate a 'Maritime Counter- Terrorism Strategy' and a 'Strategy for the Indian Ocean'.

Maritime cooperation and security would ensure secure and safe seas which in turn would allow resurgence of our economies in a mutually beneficial manner. The template of land groupings may not necessarily ap-ply to islands states. The sub- regional grouping with Maldives and Sri Lanka has to transcend beyond the South Asia sphere, encompassing

Seychelles and Mauritius and would be a 'Bottom Up Approach' to shaping the maritime strategic environment in the Indian ocean .

Endnotes

1   R K Dhowan " Indian ocean region :emerging strategic cooperation , competition and conflict scenarios", key note address ,*USI journal,* Vol. CXLIV, No. 598 2014, pp544-545 .

2   "Small Island Developing States, available", available at https://en.wikipedia. org/wiki/Small_Island_Developing_States

3   David Brewster "India: Regional net security provider", available at http:// www.gatewayhouse.in/india-regional-net-security-provider/

4   "Trilateral Maritime Security Initiative", available at http://www.mea.gov.in/ in-focus-article.htm?23037/NSA+level+meeting+on+trilateral+Maritime+Se curity+Cooperation+between+India+Sri+Lanka+and+Maldives

5   "Seychelles, Mauritius join Indian Ocean maritime security group", *The Hindu,* March 7, 2014, available at www.thehindu.com/news/national/...indian ocean.../article5758402.ece

6   "Pakistani Consulate In Colombo Was Being Used To Target", available at *http://inserbia.info/today/2014/06/pakistani-consulate-in-colombo-was-being-used-to-target-south-india/*

7   "Al-Qaeda chief Zawahiri launches al-Qaeda in South Asia", available at *www. bbc.com/news/world-asia-29056668*Sep 4, 2014

8   "Taliban storms Karachi harbour", The Dawn, March 20, 2013, available at www.dawn.com/news/11316549.

9   Al Qaeeda ,Taliban &LET have sea going skills: the attacks on USS Cole , Karachi and the 2008 Mumbai attacks are proof enough .

10 "Pakistani boat blows itself up at sea off Porbandar", *NDTV,* January 2, 2015, available at http://www.ndtv.com/india-news/pakistani-boat-blows-itself-up-at-sea-off-porbandar-721686

11 "Coast Guard seize 'suspicious' vessel off Kerala coast ", *The Indian Express,* July 6, 2015, available at http://indianexpress.com/article/india/india-others/ suspicious-vessel-caught-off-kerala-coast/

12 "Piracy off Somalia", *Indian Navy,* available at : *indiannavy.nic.in/ operations.*

13 D S Rajan, "The Unfolding China's Indian Ocean Strategy", South Asia Analysis Group, Paper No. 5646, February, 2014, available at www.southasiaanalysis. org/node/1455.

14 Ashay Abbhi, String of Pearls: India and the Geopolitics of Chinese Foreign Policy, *E-International Relations*, Jul 26, 2015, available at http://www.e-ir. info/2015/07/26/string-of-pearls-india-and-the-geopolitics-of-chinese-foreign-policy/

15 Andrew S. Erickson, Austin Strange, Austin Strange , "China's Global Maritime Presence: Hard and Soft Dimensions of PLAN Antipiracy Operations", *China Brief*, Volume: 15 Issue: 9, May 1, 2015, available at http://www.jamestown.org/ programs/chinabrief/single/?tx_ttnews[tt_news]=43868&cHash=8a087cf151 074eed214dfe5bba01edbf#.V4DFzFL7AdU

16 "Seychelles offers facilities to China", *The Guardian*, Mar 22, 2012, available at www.theguardian.com › world › china.

17 P K Ghosh, "Game Changer? Chinese submarines in the Indian ocean", *The Diplomat*, Jul 6, 2015, available at thediplomat.com/.../game-changers-Chinese-submarines-in-the-Indian-ocean.

18 Zorawar.Daulet Singh, "Indian perceptions of china's maritime silk road idea", *Journal of Defence Studies*, Vol. 8 , issue 4, Oct 2015, pp. 133-148.

19 Akhilesh Pillalamarri, "Project Mausam", *The Diplomat,* Sep 18, 2014 available at thediplomat.com/.../project-Mausam-India's-answer-to-China's-maritime-sil...

20 "The Blue Economy", *The Indian Express*, Jul 18, 2015.

21 "Operation Cactus: India's 1988 intervention in the Maldives", *The National Interest*, Apr 18, 2014, available *pragati.nationalinterest.in/.../operation-cactus-indias-1988-intervention-i...*

22 Vijay Sakhuja, "Indian Naval Diplomacy: Post Tsunami", Institute of Peace and Conflict Studies, Feb 8, 2005 , available at: www.ipcs.org/.../navy/indian-naval-diplomacy-post-tsunami-1640.html

23 Kapil Narula, "Drinking water crisis in Maldives: India leads the way", *NMF Commentary*, Jan 06 2015, available at: www.maritimeindia.org/ archives.

24 "Maldives: upgradation of Maldives airport", *Haveeru Online, available* at ***www.haveeru.com.mv/malehulhule_bridge***

25 "New land law in Maldives gives India china chills", Indian Express, Jul 23, 2015.

26 "It's the Gucci handbag of holidays': Maldives tops Chinese" South China Morning Post, January 21, 2015, available at *www.scmp.com/.../china/.../ Chinese-tourists-increasingly-be-beside-seasid..*

27 Nilanthi Samaranayake, "India's Key to Sri Lanka: Maritime Infrastructure Development" *The Diplomat Mar 31, 2015,available at http://thediplomat. com/2015/03/indias-key-to-sri-lanka-maritime-infrastructure-development/*

28 David Brewster, *India's Ocean: The Story of India's Bid for Regional Leadership*, Routledge, London, 2014.

29 "Sri Lanka wants to renew Colombo-Tuticorin ferry service" Jun 16, 2015, available at *worldmaritimenews.com/.../Sri-Lanka-wants-to-renew-Colombo-Tuticorin*

30 "Kachchatheevu was not ceded to Sri Lanka, centre tells court", *The Hindu*, Aug 31, 2013

31 "Sri Lankan deep sea trawlers fish in Indian EEZ: no country for small fishers", *The Hindu*, Nov 4, 2014

32 "Chinese fishing off Sri Lanka hits Indian fish workers" *Business Line*, Jun 24, 2013

33 "Kerala port with Adani: why that's a good" *NDTV*, Jul 13, 2015, available at: thing.*www.ndtv.com› opinion* .

34 Rohan Gunasekera, "India warns Sri Lanka over maritime security concerns", *Economy Next*, Sep 25 2015, available at http://www.economynext.com/India_warns_Sri_Lanka_over_maritime_security_concerns-3-3078-10.html

35 "Bangladesh wins another legal battle in the bay", *Dhaka Tribune*, Jul 8, 2014, available at www.dhakatribune.com/bangladesh/.../bangladesh-gets-19467-square-kilometre/.

36 Vijay Sakhuja, "India Reinforces Maritime Domain Awareness but Challenges Remain", December 2, 2014, available at http://cimsec.org/india-reinforces-maritime-domain-awareness-challenges-remain/13789

37 "India developing network of coastal radars", *Defense News*, Mar 20, 2015, available at news*www.defensenews.com/story/.../India...coastal-radar...Indian.../25084237..*

38 "India to keep an eye on shipping in Indian ocean", available at : *worldmaritimenews.com/.../India-to-keep-an-eye-on-shipping-in-Indian-*

39 "Malaysia lauds Indian navy for mh370 search efforts", *The Economic Times*, Mar 12, 2015

40 Gurpreet Khurana, "India's Yemen evacuation: an evolving doctrine", *NMF issue brief*, May 21 , 2015, available http://www.maritimeindia.org/View%20 Profile/Maritime%20Perspective%2015.pdf

41 "Sri Lanka conduct naval exercises", *The Hindu*, Sep 24, 2011

42 Jayanti, Samaranayake, "Views from India's smaller maritime Neighbours", CSIS, June 18, 2015, available at *http/amti.csis.org/views-from-India's-smaller-maritime-neighbours/*

43 "India's own string of pearls: Sri Lanka, Mauritius, Seychelles" The Lowy Institute, Mar 13, 2011, available at *www.lowyinterpreter.org/.../India's-own-string-of-pearls-Sri-Lanka-Maur*

44 "After Mauritius, India to export warships to Sri Lanka", *the Times of India*, Dec 20, 2014.

45 "Indian navy to buy 80 interception boats from Sri Lankan builder", available at *...defenceforumindia.com › forums › Indian defence › Indian Navy*

46 C. Raja Mohan, "Narendra Modi and the ocean: maritime power and responsibility" *The Indian Express*, Mar 12, 2015

47 "Indian ocean rim ocean", Oct 31 , 2015, available at: www.iora.net

48 PK Ghosh, "Indian ocean naval symposium: uniting the maritime Indian ocean region," *Strategic Analysis*, Vol36, Issue 3 2012, pp- 352-357

49 "Contact Group on Piracy off the Coast of Somalia", Available at https:// en.wikipedia.org/wiki/Contact_Group_on_Piracy_off_the_Coast_of_Somalia

50 "International Fleet Review 100 ships from 60 nations: Vizag braces for it's biggest", the Indian Express, Jul 26, 2014

51 "Apex maritime authority for coastal security" *The Times of India*, Jun 10, 2014

Chapter 13

Islamic Fundamentalism in Maldives and its Implications on Regional Cooperation

Anurag Tripathi

Strategically sensitive, Maldives is located 300 miles off the southern coast of India, having 1192 islands 199 of which are inhabited and home to 393,253 people[1]. Muslims occupy 99.41 per-cents[2] of the population of Maldives, a famous tourist destination in the Indian Ocean. Now it is yet another victim of Islamic extremism[3]in South Asia. According Combating Terrorism Center (CTC), Maldives depends upon a healthy tourist industry for its economic survival. Travel & Tourism generated 48,000 jobs directly in 2014 (32. 2% of total employment) and this is forecast to remain the same in 2015 at 48,000 (31.7% of total employment). This includes employment by hotels, travel agents, airlines and other passenger transportation services (excluding g commuter services). It also includes, for example, the activities of the restaurant and leisure industries directly supported by tourists[4]. A dramatic rise in jihadist activities and the violence that accompanies them is placing the Islands' economic wellbeing in jeopardy.[5]

Some Major incidents

In the 2008 general election, Mohamed Nasheed defeated Maumoon Abdul Gayoom, who had ruled the country for 30 over years, and established first democratic government in Maldives. Though Nasheed is Sunni Muslim, during the election campaign, Gayoom and his supporters accused Nasheed, of spreading Christianity in the Maldives. In December 2011, Nasheed and his Maldivian Democratic Party (MDP) faced massive protests, called the "Defend Islam" protests by opposition parties, extremist groups in the Male. The protesters accused the Nasheed administration of defiling Islam, arguing that Nasheed promoted Western ideals and culture and restricted the spread of more austere Islamic practices. On February 7, 2012, a bloodless coup toppled the Maldives' first democratically-elected government[6].

The state religion of Maldives is Sunni Islam. The island converted from Buddhism in the 12th century, thus the indigenous population effectively became Muslims. Since Islam was introduced in the Maldives in the 12th century, religious practices in the country have been moderate Islam. For hundreds of years, Sunni Muslims in the Maldives have largely practiced a more liberal form of the religion. However, in the past two decades, the country has grown increasingly religiously conservative. In 1994, the Protection of Religious Unity Act was passed by the Government, which restricted the freedom to practice any other religion besides Islam[7]. In 1996, Government constituted the Supreme Council for Islamic Affairs (which was renamed the Ministry of Islamic Affairs in 2008) charged with overseeing religious affairs in the country. This body of clerics pressured the government to carry out moral and cultural policing of alleged "anti-Islamic activities."[8] By the revision of the constitution in 2008: Article 9, Section D states that a non-Muslim may not become a citizen of the Maldives[9].

Significantly, by the end of Gayoom's time in office in 2008, the dress code for women had grown increasingly conservative, and more and more men grew out their beards. Ahmed Naseem, the Maldivian foreign minister until the coup in 2012, said that the Maldives "had no one wearing headscarves 10 years ago," but it is common now.[10]

Internal sleazing, by leaders, and extremist groups, with the support of external players, particularly Pakistan, Saudi Arab and China, have engendered the present unrest and instability in Maldives. Saudi and Pakistani funds have made schools, mosques and university grants available to Maldivian citizens, exposing them to more radical interpretations of familiar texts[11]. Substantial number of Maldivian nationals pursues their studies in Pakistani madras's controlled by various militants outfits and also some are enrolled in Saudi Arabian madrasas. After returning back, they are not only coming with radical ideas but also, with militant's networks. These madrsa-educated youths are influenced to fight in places like Afghanistan,

Iraq and Chechnya. They also help in the direct recruitment of Maldivians for jihad[12]. Strands of extremism and terrorism in the Maldives were visible for a long time. In 2002, Ibrahim Fauzee, a Maldivian, was arrested in Pakistan's port city of Karachi, the provincial capital of Sindh, for alleged links to the Al-Qaeda[13]. Surprisingly, on May 27, 2009, at least 27 persons were killed and 356 were injured in a suicide attack on the ISI headquarters in Lahore, Ali Jaleel, a Maldivian citizen was responsible for attack.

A major force behind more austere religious practices in the Maldives is the Adhaalath Party (Justice Party). The party supports the strict implementation of Shari`a, and it has outspokenly argued that music and singing are haram (forbidden) in Islam.[14] The party has called for an end to the sale of alcohol at the country's hundreds of luxury resorts, the only places where it is served in the country. It is widely considered the greatest force behind the Maldives' movement toward religious conservatism. Most recently, Islamic Affairs Minister Saeed, a leading member of the Adhaalath Party, has started a campaign against Christians and what he termed "Freemasons," alleging that they want to "wipe out" Islam from the Maldives.[15]

There are also two religious conservative non-governmental organizations known as Jamiyyathu Salaf (JS) and the Islamic Foundation of Maldives (IFM). These two groups, both considered Salafist, work with the country's political parties to further the cause of Islamism in the Maldives.[16] These parties and organizations were all part of the "Defend Islam" protests in December 2011, which unleashed a chain of events that culminated in the fall of Nasheed's government.

The Maldives has only experienced one terrorist attack perpetrated by Islamist terrorists. A bomb exploded in Sultan Park in Male on September 29, 2007. The explosion wounded at least 12 foreigners, including British, Japanese and Chinese tourists.[17] On February 7, 2012, a group of Islamist radicals vandalized archaeological artifacts that were mostly ancient Hindu and Buddhist relics in the National Museum. According to the museum's director, the vandals destroyed "99%" of the evidence of the Maldives' pre-Islamic history prior to the 12th century[18].

The strength of religious extremist groups lies in keeping the people poor, uneducated and unenlightened. Men from such backgrounds easily become soldiers of religious jihad. The Maldives, under the current disposition, has all the potential to become a sanctuary for jihadists. People in Maldives have links with the Al Qaeda and Pakistani organizations, like the Lashkar-e Taiba (LeT). Islamic extremism today is no longer handled by individual organizations. They have become an industry with organizations supporting each other[19]. Conspicuously, the rise of religious extremism in Maldives and the official support it has got has an enormous political and security impact on the region. The terrorist campaign, sponsored by external players and waged by Islamic fundamentalist groups in the region, has wide implications and poses a major threat to the region.

India and Maldives

India and Maldives share ethnic, linguistic, cultural, religious and commercial links steeped in antiquity and enjoy cordial and multi-dimensional relations. India was among the first to recognize Maldives after its independence in 1965 and to establish diplomatic relations with the country[20]. Since then, almost all Prime Ministers of India visited the Maldives. From the Maldivian side, former President Maumoon Abdul Gayoom and former President Mohamed Nasheed made a number of visits to India during their Presidencies. President Abdulla Yameen visited India with a high level delegation on a State visit from January 1-4, 2014, which was his first official visit abroad. He also attended the swearing-in ceremony of the Prime Minister Shri Narendra Modi in May 2014. India and Maldives have consistently supported each other in multilateral fora such as the United Nation (UN), the Commonwealth, the Non Alignment Movement (NAM) and the South Asian Association for Regional Cooperation (SAARC).

Meanwhile, India is a leading development partner of Maldives and has established many of the leading institutions of Maldives including the Indira Gandhi Memorial Hospital (IGMH), Faculty of Engineering Technology (FET) and Faculty of Hospitality & Tourism Studies (IMFFHTS). Capacity building and skills development is one of the key components of India's assistance to Maldives. India offers several scholarships to Maldivian students under the following schemes:

- ICCR scholarships

- SAARC Chair Fellowship

- ITEC training & scholarships

- Technical Cooperation Scheme of Colombo Plan

- Medical scholarships

Additionally, India is a major economic partner for the small island nation in the Indian Ocean. India and Maldives signed a trade agreement in 1981, which provides for export of essential commodities. Growing from modest beginnings, India-Maldives bilateral trade now stands at Rs.700 crores[21].

Table - 1

Bilateral Trade (in million USD)

Period	Indian Exports	Indian Imports	Total
2010	125.5	2.5	127.5
2011	147.8	2.8	150.4
2012	147.7	2.8	150.5
2013	154.0	2.3	156.3
2014	170.6	2.9	173.5

Source: Ministry of External Affairs, India- Maldives Relations (2015), *Government of India,* http://www.mea.gov.in/Portal/ForeignRelation/ MALDIVES_2015_07_02.pdf

India and Maldives share long cultural links. Three historical mosques (Friday Mosque and Dharumavantha Rasgefaanu Mosque-Male', Fenfushi Mosque-South Ari Atoll) were successfully restored by Indian experts from NRLCCP, Lucknow[22]. Bollywood films, music and television serials are very popular in Maldives. The India Cultural Center (ICC), established in Male in July 2011, conducts Regular courses in yoga, classical music and dance. ICC programmes have become immensely popular among Maldivians of all ages.

Security cooperation is a highly significant dimension of bilateral cooperation. Since the early 2000s, major increases in development cooperation have correlated closely with new security agreements. These agreements cover every sector of security, from environmental protection to terrorism. In 2009, the Indian Coast Guard has began carrying out regular sorties over Maldives to look for suspicious vessels, while the Southern Naval Command is incorporating the islands further into the Indian security grid. The November 2011 agreement that established a second Standby Credit Facility also enhanced the level of security cooperation between India and the Maldives. The two states agreed to cooperate on piracy, maritime security and terrorism, and to establish coordinated patrolling of the area. India concluded the twentieth DOSTI, meaning "friendship," naval exercise with the Maldives in April 2012, even adding Sri Lanka to the two-decade bilateral engagement. Additionally, in October 2012, India announced that it would station a defense attaché in Male and increase training of Maldivian helicopter pilots and defense personnel. Finally, in July 2013, the three countries signed an agreement to advance maritime domain awareness in the region[23].

Significantly, the Maldivian government's decision to terminate the contract of GMR India to develop the Ibrahim Nasir International Airport, and subsequent internal political developments in Maldives led to strain in their relations. In response to Indian government froze its US$25 million aid to the island nation.

Recently, on October 11, 2015, India and the Maldives discussed cooperation in defence and security, trade and connectivity and health among other issues during the visit of external affairs minister Sushma Swaraj for the 5th Joint Commission meeting. Sushma Swaraj emphasised the Indian government's policy of "neighbours first", as Yameen underscored the need to cement India-Maldives relations further, said an official statement. Yameen conveyed that Maldives would hold an Investment Forum in India in 2016, which is also the 'Visit Maldives' year. He reiterated the Maldives' policy of 'India First'. The defense and security relationship was part of the forward looking discussions in the Joint Commission for the first time India-Maldives defense cooperation includes, inter-alia, the construction of a Composite Training Centre for the Maldivian National Defense Forces (MNDF), joint patrolling, training programmes for MNDF officers in India, medical camps, joint exercises, etc, the statement said. The two countries were of the view that the bilateral partnership was important also for maintaining security in the Indian Ocean Region. Both sides agreed on an early finalization to the Mutual Legal Assistance Treaty in criminal matters. The Maldives reiterated its strong support to India's candidature as a permanent member of the UN Security Council.[24]

A stable and moderate Muslim state at the heart of the Indian Ocean would prove a welcome ally in defusing regional tensions. In March 2015, Mohamed Nasheed the man who was fought for democracy sentenced to jail for 13 years. There have been radicalised Maldivians who have joined in ISIS. According to the Commissioner of Maldivian Police, Hussein Waheed, there over 50 Maldivians have been known to be fighting foreign wars. However, the MDP claims that there are about 200. The worrisome factor is that these reported jihadists have been young men and/or couples with infants who travel to Syria via Turkey making false excuses about their journey[25].

Significantly, Maldivian-origin extremists have in the past carried out their activities in the southern states of India. Moosa Inas, a prime suspect in the 2005 Sultan Park case had travelled to Pakistan via Kerala. Asif Ibrahim, another Maldivian captured in Kerala was there to start a new Maldives-based terror group in Thiruvananthapuram, capital of Kerala. Given the geographical proximity the two countries share, the rise in the number of Maldivians joining extremist groups is a security concern for India. Besides, stability of the Maldives is strategically significant for India also because of the increasing Chinese influence in the island-nation[26].

Importantly, Jamaat-ul-Muslimeen, a new Maldives-based terror outfit, having links with the Lashkar-e Toiba (LeT) was the mastermind of an attack in Male in 2007 in which 12 foreign tourists were injured in Sultan Park near the Islamic Centre. India is also worried from the infiltration of Indian terror group Students Islamic Movement of India (SIMI) to Maldives, especially after its crackdown in India. The previous government of Mohammed Nasheed resorted to some measures to tone down the radicalization through regulating local madrasa and seminaries. The island-state is also not too far from India's southern coast making it an ideal launch pad for attacks through sea. The LeT has plans to use the Maldivian islands as storehouses for weapons and explosives and use them as a launch pad against attack on India[27].

India has been quick when Maldives has faced any crisis. While India cannot directly help Maldives combat the problem of radicalization, it can provide more educational opportunities and security assistance along with the rest of the international community. The balance of not pressurizing the country into feeling controlled by the international community but still voicing concern and seriousness over the issues is tricky but needs to be achieved. In the past two decades, Maldivians in increasing numbers have been drawn towards Pakistan-based madrasa and jihadist groups. Lack of adequate educational and employment opportunities have been pushing the Maldivian youth towards jihadist groups and other violent gangs.[28]

Relations between India and the Maldives have had their highs and low. Security cooperation is a highly significant dimension of bilateral cooperation— India has, for example, helped the Maldives set up its coastal surveillance capabilities. Additionally, India is a major economic partner for the small island nation in the Indian Ocean[29]. The presence of any global or regional powers in Maldives would facilitate it in gaining supremacy of Indian Ocean which could pose a serious threat to the security and integrity of the region as well as India.

The various threats that can manifest themselves as terrorist activities in Maldives need to be examined in their various dimensions. The best counter-terrorism option for Maldives is to establish better understanding and cooperation with the international community especially regional countries. Counter-terrorism strategy should closely work not only within internal institutions but also with other countries. A feasible policy in countering terrorism is to defeat terrorism through international partnerships. Maldivian government must also be committed to implement the United Nations Global Counterterrorism Strategy. An integrated and comprehensive approach should be the preferred tool for countering the threat of terrorism in the Maldives in the future.

Cooperation between India and Maldives is very significant for the security of the South Asia region. The existence of any terror outfit bases or breeding grounds for terrorism in the Indian neighbourhood would be a threat to regional security as well as Indian security. The need for structured counter-terrorism cooperation between the two countries is the need of the hour. Counter-terrorism training and capacity building, handing over of fugitives, sharing of intelligence, investigative assistance, joint-patrolling and maritime security are some areas where we can cooperate to each other and avoid any volatile consequences.

Conclusion

Maldives has recently become a potential fertile ground for Islamic fundamentalism. Its geographical location, political instability, illiteracy and dependence of fellow Muslim countries for economic growth have compounded the situation. Indeed external funding particularly from Pakistan and Saudi Arab, and some of these funds are channelized through extremist groups, have engendered the present unrest and instability in Maldives. Maldivians dependence on external education system especially in Pakistani madras's who are controlled by various militants' outfits and also some are enrolled in Saudi Arabian madras's create more internal problem as they are not only coming with radical ideas but also, with militant's networks. These radicalized groups conduct terrorist activities along with other foreign nationals in different parts of the world.

In order to avoid these radicals groups work with anti-India dispensations against Indian interest, India needs to make soft power approach towards the island nations. Since culturally and geographically Maldives closer to India, it will not be a difficult propensity to turn the focus against India. So India has to ensure that with close cooperation with the Maldivian government Maldivians get modern and liberal education and the people who have gone for education abroad are not coming back with radicalism. Similarly, India Maldives political cooperation also needs to be strengthened so that China would not become a closer security partner for Maldives.

Endnotes

1   "The World Fact Book (2015)", *Central Inteligence Agency*, available at: https://www.cia.gov/library/publications/the-world-factbook/geos/mv.html

2   *Minivan News* (2010),   December 10, 2015, available at : http://minivannewsarchive.com/society/maldives-a-99-41-percent-muslim-country-claims-rissc-report-10838

3   Singh RSN (2012), "Strategic Significance of Maldives", *Indian Defence Review*, December 13, 2015, available at: http://www.indiandefencereview.com/spotlights/strategic-significance-of-maldives/

4   "World Travell and Tourism council" (2015), available at: https://www.wttc.org//media/files/reports/economic%20impact%20research/countries%20 2015/maldives2015.pdf

5   Roul Animesh (2013), "The Threat from Rising Extremism in the Maldives", *ETH Zuritch*, November 15, 2015, available at : http://www.isn.ethz.ch/Digital-Library/Articles/Detail/?id=163176

6   Ibid

7   "2010 Report on International Religious Freedom – Maldives," *United Nations*, November 17, 2010.

8   "Ministry Asks Police to Ban Discos," *Minivan News*, December 31, 2008.

9   "Islam in Maldives," November 5, 2015, available at : https://en.wikipedia.org/wiki/Islam_in_the_Maldives , accessed on

10 Wright, The "Defend Islam" banners displayed slogans such as "We stand united for Islam and the nation," "No idols in this holy land," "No to the Zionist murderers," and "No to El Al (Israeli) Airlines."

11 Iman Mariyad (2013), "The rise of radical Islam in the Maldives" *Blog Active*, available at : https://imadmariyam.blogactiv.eu/2013/09/16/maldives-islam/

12 Manoharan N (2014), "An Agenda for the New Government: Policy Options for India in Maldives", *IPCS* , November 10, 2015, available at: http://www.ipcs.org/issue-brief/south-asia/an-agenda-for-the-new-government-policy-options-for-india-250.html

13 Roy Bhaskar (2013), "Maldives Turning Into a Terrorist Haven", *South Asia Analysis Group*, December 12, 2015, available at : http://www.southasiaanalysis.org/node/1285

14 "No One Has the Right to Criticise the Rulings of the Islamic Sharia – Adhaalath," Miadhu, March 1, 2013; "Adhaalath Party Requests Education Ministry Cancel Inter-School Singing Competition," Minivan News, April 12, 2012; "Adhaalath was Formed to Work Against the Anti-Religious Activities of MDP – Imran," Miadhu, January 29, 2013.

15 "Islamic Ministry Claims Christians, Freemasons Secretly Working to 'Eradicate' Islam in the Maldives," *Minivan News*, February 12, 2013.

16 "Ibrahim Fauzee – The Guantanamo Docket," *New York Times*, undated; "Maldives Offers to Take Two Guantanamo Bay Prisoners," *Agence France-Presse*, May 16, 2010.

17 "Bomb Blast Injures 12 Tourists in Maldives," *Reuters*, September 30, 2007.

18 "Footage Leaked of Museum Vandals Destroying Pre-Islamic Artifacts," *Minivan News*, January 14, 2013.

19 Roy Bhaskar (2013), "Maldives Turning Into a Terrorist Haven", *South Asia Analysis Group*, December 12, 2015, available at: http://www.southasiaanalysis. org/node/1285

20 " India- Maldives Relations" (2015), *MEA*, available at: http://www.mea.gov.in/ Portal/ForeignRelation/MALDIVES_2015_07_02.pdf

21 Ibid

22 Ibid

23 Cody M. Poplin (2013), " India-Maldives Bilateral Brief," *IDCR*, available at : http://idcr.cprindia.org/blog/india-maldives-bilateral-brief

24 " India, Maldives to step up cooperation in defence, security" (2015), *Hindustan Times*, Oct 11, 2015.

25 Thomas Roshni (2015), "Radicalism in the Maldives: Should India be worried?," *IPCS* , available at: http://www.ipcs.org/article/terrorism/radicalism-in-the-maldives-should-india-be-worried-4888.html ,

26 Ibid

27 "India Maldives Bilateral Relations," available: http://www.gktoday.in/india-maldives-bilateral-relations/

28 Rishan, Ahmed, "Rate of unemployment rises to 28 percent in the Maldives," Haveeru, 10 May 2010.

29 Panda Ankit (2015), "India's Maldivian Headache", *The Diplomat*, February 26, 2015, available: http://thediplomat.com/2015/02/indias-maldivian-headache/

Index

www.ingramcontent.com/pod-product-compliance
Lightning Source LLC
Chambersburg PA
CBHW030332270326
41926CB00010B/1589